总 策 划：许　琳

总 监 制：夏建辉　王君校

监　　 制：韩　晖　张彤辉　顾　蕾　刘根芹

主　　 编：吴中伟

编　 者：吴中伟　吴叔平　高顺全　吴金利

修　　 订：吴中伟

顾　 问：陶黎铭　陈光磊

Dāngdài Zhōngwén

当代中文
修订版

Contemporary Chinese
Revised Edition

Kèběn

课本

1

TEXTBOOK
Volume One

主　编：吴中伟

编　者：吴中伟　吴叔平

　　　　高顺全　吴金利

翻　译：徐　蔚

　　　　Yvonne L. Walls　Jan W. Walls

译文审校：Jerry Schmidt

First Edition 2003

Revised Edition 2014

Seventh Printing 2019

ISBN 978-7-5138-0617-6

Copyright 2014 by Confucius Institute Headquarters (Hanban)

Published by Sinolingua Co., Ltd

24 Baiwanzhuang Road, Beijing 100037, China

Tel: (86)10-68320585, 68997826

Fax: (86)10-68997826, 68326333

http://www.sinolingua.com.cn

E-mail: hyjx@sinolingua.com.cn

Facebook: www.facebook.com/sinolingua

Printed by Beijing Mixing Printing Co. Ltd.

Printed in the People's Republic of China

User's Guide to the Revised Edition

The Chinese language learning course book series *Contemporary Chinese* is designed around the basis of grammatical structure and is integrated with differing topics, functions and cultural aspects. This series is aimed at developing students' comprehensive skills of listening to, speaking, reading and writing Chinese. It includes *Textbooks* volumes one through four, with an accompanying *Exercise Book* and *Teacher's Book* for each, audio materials as well as a *Character Book* for Volume 1 and Volume 2.

The first edition of *Contemporary Chinese* was published in 2003. The series is now in its revised edition and has been modified based on suggestions from readers worldwide (HSK) and taking into consideration the Chinese Proficiency Test Syllabus and the International Curriculum for Chinese Language Education. This edition retains many features from the first edition, with some mistakes corrected and part of the texts updated. Some exercises and activities have been added in the *Textbooks* while *Testing Materials* and *Supplementary Reading Materials* will be offered for this edition.

Features of this series:

1. Elementary-level instruction: Equal importance should be attached to conversation, phonetics and Chinese characters, and a systematic approach should be taken to teach these three aspects independently. Phonetics is the key to speech and thus will become the teaching focus at the elementary level; while Chinese characters are the stepping stone to reading and writing, characters should be taught beginning with basic strokes and stroke orders and a few characters with typical structures so as to cultivate a sense of their overall structure in students. Conversation should be taught by asking students to repeat full sentences after listening. We suggest that 1/5 of a class period be spent in teaching conversation, 3/5 training phonetics and 1/5 practicing characters successively so that this course will not only help students to create a solid foundation of phonetics and Chinese characters, but also satisfy their communication desire, break the normal learning routine and help them to acquire a sense of achievement.

2. Phonetic instruction: At the elementary-level, phonetic teaching should be carried out from an overview of the subject to details, then back to an overview. In this way, students can, at the outset, obtain a full picture of Chinese phonetics, then a focus may be put on training students' pronunciation step by step, then finally having the students review what they have learned. Despite all the phonemes being listed in the textbook, a concentration on teaching difficult phonemes should be made instead of putting equal focus on all. Translations are given for corresponding pinyin vocabulary words so as to reduce the monotony of memorizing meaningless phonetic units. The textbook combines the teaching of syllables and phonemes with that of speech flow. Instruction may begin from syllable to phoneme so as to improve accuracy of the latter, or from syllable to speech flow so as to reveal the functions and changes of phonetics during vernacular discourse. Phonetic teaching is a long-term task; therefore, phonetic training remains a major part of the textbook after the elementary level.

3. Chinese Character instruction: The *Character Book,* for Volumes 1 and 2 of the textbook series, is designed based on the unique features of Chinese characters to improve teaching effectiveness. In the series we will shift from the traditional method of requiring students to recognize and write characters simultaneously to the method of separating the two processes; first reading, and later writing at the elementary level. After the elementary level, we will continue to distinguish these two processes by only requiring students to be able to read and write around 25 characters per unit. By the end of Volume 2, students will possess the competence to simultaneously read and write Chinese characters. At this stage, character exercises need to be strengthened while stories related to characters can be told so as to stimulate students' interest in learning and help them to better memorize and understand Chinese.

4. Vocabulary instruction: The vocabulary in this series can be used independently of other segments. They are organized in a practical and systematic way with special exercises designed around them. The words in the glossaries of Volumes 1 and 2 are arranged based on the intrinsic meaning of or grammatical functions between words instead of their order of appearance in the text. Some of the words in the glossary do not appear in text. For example, only the character 女 appears in the text, but the glossary will contain both 女 and 男. In addition, the course series places a premium on the instruction of morphemes and adopts the teaching method of combining characters into words or associating words with characters. In *Character Book*, the meaning of morphemes for certain words is presented and then combined with previously learned characters

to form new words so as to expand students' vocabulary.

5. Grammar instruction: This series keeps the grammar to the simplest level, and focuses on the application of grammar and the learning habits of non-native learners. One approach adopted is to treat grammar points as the usages of words or phrases. For instance, the series does not list the modal verb as a grammar point as in its earlier edition. Instead, the similarities and differences between two modal verbs 能 and 会 are introduced. Another approach is to bypass some grammar points such as complex sentences and introduce correlatives as new words such as 可是 and 所以 at an early stage. Students will learn the new words first and the grammar later. The grammar points included in the book are sequenced according to their levels of difficulty and are reinforced at various stages. Many exercises are provided to train students' ability to translate the grammatical knowledge into a functional command of the language. Grammar terms are kept at a minimal level and more semantic and pragmatic explanations are provided. More detailed grammar points and some grammar related questions are included in the *Teacher's Book* for the benefit of the teachers.

6. Culture instruction: This series emphasizes everyday life, trends of the current age and contemporary issues, and features cultural differences and common grounds to make Chinese more relatable to students. The texts combine information about China and learners' native countries, with a focus on the former. Traditional culture and contemporary society are both covered, with a focus on the latter.

7. Exercises and activities: *Textbooks* are composed of different units. In Volumes 1 and 2, each unit is divided into three parts. Texts are the core of the first two parts and each text is preceded by certain warm-up activities, vocabulary exercises as well as grammar exercises. Such a scaffolding of activities and exercises are a manifestation of the teaching process aimed at examining students' preview of the vocabulary and familiarizing them with words and expressions as well as key grammar points. Furthermore, each text is followed by corresponding questions designed to check students' understanding along with certain extension tasks so as to cater to the various needs of students, which makes the series more adaptable to individual users. Language points and cultural notes constitute the third part of each unit. Cultural notes are provided for general reading while language points can be seen as a summary of the unit's key teaching points. These language points should be integrated into the course lesson plans; teachers can also use these language points to give error correcting feedback to students through the exercises.

The *Exercise Book* supplements the *Textbook*. The listening and reading exercises in the *Exercise Book* are designed to include some new words. Students are not expected to learn them as they will not affect their ability to answer the questions. This arrangement allows students to familiarize themselves with authentic communication scenarios and enhance their ability to communicate with the Chinese people in real life.

8. Teaching plans: Each volume of this series is divided into 12 units and it is suggested that 6-8 class periods be spent on each unit (Volume 1 contains eight units preceded by Unit 0, which is a preparation unit that can be covered over 24 class periods). Thus, each volume will take one semester or a school year to complete depending on the weekly class hour arrangement of the course and the level of students.

For more information regarding the basic structure and compiling thought of the series, as well as other reference materials, background information and teaching advice, please refer to the *Teacher's Book*.

We are always grateful for any of your suggestions and advice.

Wu Zhongwei

wuzhongwei@fudan.edu.cn

To the Learner

Welcome to *Contemporary Chinese*!

Contemporary Chinese is designed for students whose native language is English. The ultimate goal of this series is to develop the student's ability to comprehend and communicate in the Chinese language. Specifically, it provides training in the skills of listening, speaking, reading, and writing Chinese.

The whole series consists of **four volumes**. You may work through the whole series or use only the volumes of your choice.

The following are to be used together with the **Textbook**:

* **Exercise Book**

* **Character Book (only for Volume One and Volume Two)**

* **Audio Materials and CD-ROM**

* **Teacher's Book**

* **Testing Materials**

* **Supplementary Reading Materials**

The **Textbook**:

➤ is concise, practical, authentic, and topical,

➤ is adaptable to the varied needs of different students,

➤ gives equal attention to listening, speaking, reading, and writing,

➤ guides your learning step by step.

After working through **Volume One**, you should have a good command of **337 Chinese words and expressions, 317 Chinese characters, 27 grammar items and 23 communicative function items**, and thus have a basic command of Chinese.

Learning Chinese is not so hard.

Let's start!

你好!	Nǐ hǎo!	Hello!
你好!	Nǐ hǎo!	Hello!
谢谢!	Xièxie!	Thank you!
不客气。	Bú kèqi.	You are welcome.
对不起!	Duìbuqǐ!	I'm sorry.
没关系。	Méi guānxi.	That's all right.
再见!	Zàijiàn!	Goodbye!
再见!	Zàijiàn!	Goodbye!

Shàng kè.	Class begins.
Xià kè.	Class is over.
Xiànzài xiūxi yíxià.	Now let's have a rest.
Xiànzài jìxù shàng kè.	Now let's continue.
Qǐng dǎkāi shū, fāndào dì-sān yè.	Open your books and turn to page 3, please.
Qǐng tīng lùyīn.	Listen to the recording, please.
Qǐng gēn wǒ dú.	Read after me, please.
Qǐng zài shuō yí biàn.	Say it again, please.
Zhè shì shénme yìsi?	What does this mean?
… (Hànyǔ) zěnme shuō?	How do you say… in Chinese?
… (Hànzì) zěnme xiě?	How do you write…?
Qǐng dú yíxià.	Read it, please.
Qǐng xiě yíxià.	Write it, please.
Qǐng fānyì yíxià.	Translate it, please.
Duì bu duì?	Is it right?
Duì.	Yes, it is. / It's right.
Bú duì.	No, it isn't. / It's not right.
Qǐng kàn hēibǎn.	Look at the blackboard, please.
Xiànzài tīngxiě.	Let's have a dictation now.
Xiànzài zuò liànxí.	Let's do exercises now.
Jīntiān de zuòyè shì …	Today's homework is…

Chinese Grammar Terms

noun	N.	míngcí	名词
place word	PW	chùsuǒcí	处所词
time word	TW	shíjiāncí	时间词
location word	LW	fāngwèicí	方位词
pronoun	Pron.	dàicí	代词
question word	QW	yíwèncí	疑问词
verb	V.	dòngcí	动词
directional verb	DV	qūxiàng dòngcí	趋向动词
modal verb	MV	néngyuàn dòngcí	能愿动词
adjective	Adj.	xíngróngcí	形容词
numeral	Num.	shùcí	数词
measure word	MW	liàngcí	量词
adverb	Adv.	fùcí	副词
preposition	Prep.	jiècí	介词
conjunction	Conj.	liáncí	连词
particle	Part.	zhùcí	助词
interjection	Interj.	tàncí	叹词
subject	Subj.	zhǔyǔ	主语
predicate	Pred.	wèiyǔ	谓语
object	Obj.	bīnyǔ	宾语
attributive	Attrib.	dìngyǔ	定语
complement	Comple.	bǔyǔ	补语
adverbial	Adverbial	zhuàngyǔ	状语

People in the Text

There is a famous university named Lincoln University, in a beautiful city on the west coast of North America. Young people from different countries study there:

Bái Xiǎohóng
白小红
female, Chinese

Wáng Yīng
王英
female, Chinese Canadian

Jiāng Shān
江山
male, American

Mǎdīng
马丁
male, Australian

They have a Chinese teacher who always pretends not to know English when in the class:

Zhāng Lín
张林
male, Chinese, over forty

There are several friends who work in companies:

Dīng Hànshēng
丁汉生
male, Chinese, who
was sent to work here
by a Chinese company

Jiékè
杰克
male, Canadian, who is
an employee of an export
company and often goes to
China on business

And one more, currently in the UK:

Zhāng Yuányuan
张园园
female, Briton of Chinese
origin, Jiang Shan's
girlfriend, a student at the
Eastern College in England

Unit 0

Rùmén
入 门
Preparation

0.1

语音概要 Yǔyīn Gàiyào **Introduction to Phonetics**

音节结构 Yīnjié Jiégòu **Structure of syllables**

In Chinese, a syllable is composed of an initial (Shēngmǔ), a final (Yùnmǔ) and a tone (Shēngdiào).

Shēngdiào tone	
Shēngmǔ initial	Yùnmǔ final

e.g. mā

Here m is the initial (Shēngmǔ) and ɑ is the final (Yùnmǔ), and above the final is the tone-mark.

A syllable may consist of a final and a tone only.

e.g. à

声母 Shēngmǔ **Initials**

b   p   m   f   d   t   n   l

g   k   h   j   q   x

zh   ch   sh   r   z   c   s

韵母 Yùnmǔ **Finals**

	i	u	ü
a	ia	ua	
o		uo	
e	ie		üe
-i			
er			
ai		uai	
ei		uei (ui)	
ao	iao		
ou	iou (iu)		
an	ian	uan	üan
en	in	uen (un)	ün
ang	iang	uang	
eng	ing	ueng	
ong	iong		

声调 Shēngdiào **Tones**

第一声	dì-yī shēng	the first tone	–	55
第二声	dì-èr shēng	the second tone	´	35
第三声	dì-sān shēng	the third tone	ˇ	214
第四声	dì-sì shēng	the fourth tone	ˋ	51

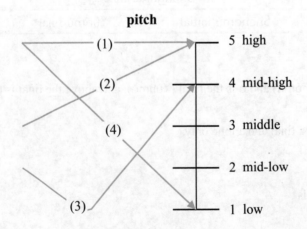

文化点 Wénhuà Diǎn **Cultural notes**

Hànyǔ Pīnyīn (The Chinese Phonetic System) is used as the Romanization system in this set of textbooks. Since the beginning of the 20th century, people who work with the Chinese language have designed several systems of phonetic symbols to deal with the fact that Chinese characters do not fully represent their pronunciation. The more important systems are the "Zhuyin Phonetic Alphabet (Zhùyīn Zìmǔ)", the "Guoyu Romanization System (Guóyǔ Luómǎzì)" and the "New Latinized Writing (Lādīnghuà Xīnwénzì)," etc. The "Chinese Phonetic System (Hànyǔ Pīnyīn Fāng'àn)", abbreviated "pīnyīn", was first published in 1958. This system has already been adopted by the United Nations and many other international organizations for spelling the Chinese language, and Chinese names. It has replaced many of the other systems and is widely used both inside and outside China.

ZPA	CPA	IPA	ZPA	CPA	IPA	ZPA	CPA	IPA
ㄅ	b	[p]	帀	-i(前)	[ɿ]	ㄧㄣ	in	[in]
ㄆ	p	[p']	帀	-i（后）	[ʅ]	ㄧㄤ	iang	[iɑŋ]
ㄇ	m	[m]	ㄧ	i	[i]	ㄧㄥ	ing	[iŋ]
ㄈ	f	[f]	ㄨ	u	[u]	ㄨㄚ	ua	[uA]
万	v	[v]	ㄩ	ü	[y]	ㄨㄛ	uo	[uo]
ㄉ	d	[t]	ㄚ	a	[A]	ㄨㄞ	uai	[uai]
ㄊ	t	[t']	ㄛ	o	[o]	ㄨㄟ	uei	[uei]
ㄋ	n	[n]	ㄜ	e	[ɤ]	ㄨㄢ	uan	[uan]
ㄌ	l	[l]	ㄝ	ê	[ɛ]	ㄨㄣ	uen	[uən]
ㄍ	g	[k]	ㄦ	er	[ɚ]	ㄨㄤ	uang	[uɑŋ]
ㄎ	k	[k']	ㄞ	ai	[ai]	ㄨㄥ	ueng	[uəŋ]
兀	ng	[ŋ]	ㄟ	ei	[ei]	ㄨㄥ	ong	[uŋ]
ㄏ	h	[x]	ㄠ	ao	[au]	ㄩㄝ	üe	[yɛ]
ㄐ	j	[tɕ]	ㄡ	ou	[ou]	ㄩㄢ	üan	[yɛn]
ㄑ	q	[tɕ']	ㄢ	an	[an]	ㄩㄣ	ün	[yn]
（广）		[ȵ]	ㄣ	en	[ən]	ㄩㄥ	iong	[yŋ]
ㄒ	x	[ɕ]	ㄤ	ang	[ɑŋ]			
ㄓ	zh	[tʂ]	ㄥ	eng	[əŋ]			
ㄔ	ch	[tʂ']	ㄧㄚ	ia	[iA]			
ㄕ	sh	[ʂ]	ㄧㄝ	ie	[iɛ]			
ㄖ	r	[ʐ]	ㄧㄠ	iao	[iau]			
ㄗ	z	[ts]	ㄧㄡ	iou	[iou]			
ㄘ	c	[ts']	ㄧㄢ	ian	[iɛn]			
ㄙ	s	[s]						

附 2

Appendix II

普通话声韵配合总表
Table of Syllables in Chinese

Initial\Final	-i[ɿ,ʅ]	a	o	e	er	ai	ei	ao	ou	an	en	ang	eng	ong	i	ia	ie	iao	iou	ian	in	iang	ing	iong	u	ua	uo	uai	uei	uan	uen	uang	ueng	ü	üe	üan	ün
b		ba	bo			bai	bei	bao		ban	ben	bang	beng		bi		bie	biao		bian	bin		bing		bu												
p		pa	po			pai	pei	pao	pou	pan	pen	pang	peng		pi		pie	piao		pian	pin		ping		pu												
m		ma	mo	me		mai	mei	mao	mou	man	men	mang	meng		mi		mie	miao	miu	mian	min		ming		mu												
f		fa	fo				fei		fou	fan	fen	fang	feng												fu												
d		da		de		dai	dei	dao	dou	dan	den	dang	deng	dong	di		die	diao	diu	dian			ding		du		duo		dui	duan	dun						
t		ta		te		tai		tao	tou	tan		tang	teng	tong	ti		tie	tiao		tian			ting		tu		tuo		tui	tuan	tun						
n		na		ne		nai	nei	nao	nou	nan	nen	nang	neng	nong	ni		nie	niao	niu	nian	nin	niang	ning		nu		nuo			nuan				nü	nüe		
l		la	lo	le		lai	lei	lao	lou	lan		lang	leng	long	li	lia	lie	liao	liu	lian	lin	liang	ling		lu		luo			luan	lun			lü	lüe		
g		ga		ge		gai	gei	gao	gou	gan	gen	gang	geng	gong											gu	gua	guo	guai	gui	guan	gun	guang					
k		ka		ke		kai		kao	kou	kan	ken	kang	keng	kong											ku	kua	kuo	kuai	kui	kuan	kun	kuang					
h		ha		he		hai	hei	hao	hou	han	hen	hang	heng	hong											hu	hua	huo	huai	hui	huan	hun	huang					
j															ji	jia	jie	jiao	jiu	jian	jin	jiang	jing	jiong										ju	jue	juan	jun
q															qi	qia	qie	qiao	qiu	qian	qin	qiang	qing	qiong										qu	que	quan	qun
x															xi	xia	xie	xiao	xiu	xian	xin	xiang	xing	xiong										xu	xue	xuan	xun
zh	zhi	zha		zhe		zhai	zhei	zhao	zhou	zhan	zhen	zhang	zheng	zhong											zhu	zhua	zhuo	zhuai	zhui	zhuan	zhun	zhuang					
ch	chi	cha		che		chai		chao	chou	chan	chen	chang	cheng	chong											chu	chua	chuo	chuai	chui	chuan	chun	chuang					
sh	shi	sha		she		shai	shei	shao	shou	shan	shen	shang	sheng												shu	shua	shuo	shuai	shui	shuan	shun	shuang					
r	ri			re				rao	rou	ran	ren	rang	reng	rong											ru		ruo		rui	ruan	run						
z	zi	za		ze		zai	zei	zao	zou	zan	zen	zang	zeng	zong											zu		zuo		zui	zuan	zun						
c	ci	ca		ce		cai		cao	cou	can	cen	cang	ceng	cong											cu		cuo		cui	cuan	cun						
s	si	sa		se		sai		sao	sou	san	sen	sang	seng	song											su		suo		sui	suan	sun						
		a	o	e	er	ai	ei	ao	ou	an	en	ang	eng		yi	ya	ye	yao	you	yan	yin	yang	ying	yong	wu	wa	wo	wai	wei	wan	wen	wang	weng	yu	yue	yuan	yun

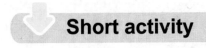

Short activity

Read aloud the following syllables. Ask your teacher to listen to your pronunciation and point out your problems. Which do you think is difficult to pronounce? Circle them.

dùzi	tùzi	shuìjiào	shuǐjiǎo
qǐngwèn	qīnwěn	zǐdàn	jīdàn
shǎoshù	xiǎoshù	zìjǐ	cíqì
yóuyù	měinǚ	fǎlǜ	xuéxí
xuǎnjǔ	chūqù	pángbiān	pànbié
shàngchuán	xióngzhuàng	jiāngjūn	zhèngzhì
jīngjì	cānguān	kuānkuò	jiéhūn
niúròu	shēngrì	rè'ài	chàng gē
zhèr	wǒmen		

0.2

A:　Nǐ　hǎo!
　　you fine
　　Hello!

B:　Nǐ　hǎo!
　　you fine
　　Hello!

A:　Nǐ　jiào　shénme míngzi?
　　you call　what　　name
　　What's your name?

B:　Wǒ jiào …　　　　Nǐ ne?
　　I　call　　　　　you *a particle*

My name is ...   And you? (= What's yours?)

A: Wǒ jiào ...
    I   call
    My name is ...

*   *   *   *

A: Lǎoshī, nín hǎo!
    Teacher you fine
    (honorific form)
    Hello, teacher!

B: Nǐ hǎo!
    you fine
    Hello!

A: Nín guìxìng?
    you be surnamed
    (honorific form)
    What's your surname?

B: Wǒ xìng …　　　　　Nǐ ne?

　　I　be surnamed　　you *a particle*

　　My surname is …　　And you?

A: Wǒ xìng …　　　　　Wǒ jiào …

　　I　be surnamed　　　I　call

　　My surname is …　　My name is …

　　　　　　　　＊　　＊　　＊　　＊

A: Nǐ shì nǎ guó rén?

　　you be which country person

　　What's your nationality?

B: Wǒ shì … rén.　　Nǐ ne?

　　I　be　person　you *a particle*

　　I am from …　　　And you?

A: Wǒ shì … rén.

　　I　be　person

　　I am from …

Activity

Role play: Ask each other's name and nationality. Try to say your country's name in Chinese and say your Chinese name if you have one.

Words for reference:

xìng　　one's family name

jiào　　to call, to name

shì　　to be

语音　Yǔyīn　Phonetics

声母和韵母　Shēngmǔ hé Yùnmǔ　Initials and finals

a	o	e	yi (= i)	wu (= u)	yu (= ü)
ba	bo		bi	bu	
pa	po		pi	pu	
ma	mo		mi	mu	

fa	fo		fu	
da		de	di	du
ta		te	ti	tu
na		ne	ni	nu	nü
la		le	li	lu	lü

Notes:

1. yi wu yu

   When standing as syllables by themselves, the finals i, u, ü are written as yi, wu, yu.

2. o e

   What distinguishes o and e is that the former is pronounced with the lips rounded and the latter is pronounced with the lips in a neutral position. (see picture)

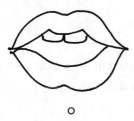 

o　　　　　　　　　　e

3. ü

   Chinese ü is like French *u*, e.g. *sur* or German *ü*, e.g. *über*. It can be formed by rounding the lips as for [u:] (as in *too*, *food*) and then pronouncing [i:] (as in *eat*, *peak*).

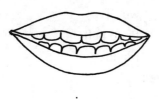 

i　　　　　　　　　　ü

声调 Shēngdiào **Tones**

ˉ	第一声	dì-yī shēng	the first tone
´	第二声	dì-èr shēng	the second tone
ˇ	第三声	dì-sān shēng	the third tone
`	第四声	dì-sì shēng	the fourth tone

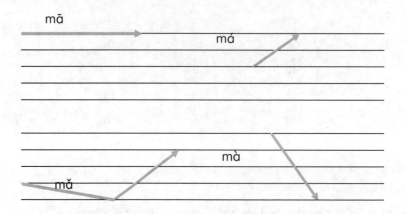

The tone refers to the pitch variation within a syllable.

Syllables of different tones often have different meanings, e.g.

mā mother   mǎ horse

má hemp   mà abuse, curse

Do the phonemes a, o, e, i, u, ü, b, p, m, f, d, t, n, l exist in your native language? If so, please give an example. If not, try to find a similar one and explain their differences.

Read aloud the following words.

bā eight	bà father	pá to climb	pà be afraid of
dà big	dǎ to hit	tā he/she/it	tǎ pagoda
mā mother	mǎ horse	wǔ five	wù fog
è hungry	é goose	lā to pull	là spicy
ná to take, to carry	nǎ which	nà that	
fó Buddha	pò broken, torn, damaged		
nǔlì (work) hard	fǎlǜ law		
dà yǔ heavy rain	dàyī overcoat		

0.3

会话 Huìhuà **Conversation**

A: Nǐ xuéxí shénme?
you study what
What are you studying?

B: Wǒ xuéxí Hànyǔ. Nǐ ne?
I study Chinese (language) you *a particle*
I am studying Chinese. And you?

A: Wǒ yě xuéxí Hànyǔ.
I also study Chinese (language)
I am studying Chinese too.

*   *   *   *

A: Hànyǔ zěnmeyàng?

Chinese how

What do you think of Chinese?

B: Hànyǔ hěn yǒu yìsi.

Chinese very have meaning (interest)

Chinese is interesting.

A: Nán bu nán?

difficult not difficult

(Is it) Difficult?

B: Bú tài nán.

not too difficult

(It's) Not too difficult.

*   *   *   *

A: Nǐ xuéxí shénme?

you study what

What are you studying?

B: Wǒ xuéxí Hànyǔ.

I study Chinese (language)

I am studying Chinese.

A: Nǐ zài nǎr xuéxí Hànyǔ?

you in/at where study Chinese

Where are you studying Chinese?

B: Wǒ zài … xuéxí Hànyǔ. Nǐ ne?

I in/at study Chinese you *a particle*

I am studying Chinese in … And you?

B: Wǒ zài Zhōngguó xuéxí Yīngyǔ.

I in/at China study English

I am studying English in China.

Activity

Role play: Ask each other what language he/she is studying and how he/she feels about it.

Words for reference:

nán	difficult
róngyì	easy
yǒu yìsi	interesting, fun
méi / méiyǒu yìsi	not interesting; no fun

 语音　Yǔyīn　**Phonetics**

声母和韵母　Shēngmǔ hé Yùnmǔ　**Initials and finals**

ai	ei	ao	ou	an	en	ang	eng	ong
gai	gei	gao	gou	gan	gen	gang	geng	gong
kai	kei	kao	kou	kan	ken	kang	keng	kong
hai	hei	hao	hou	han	hen	hang	heng	hong

Notes:

1.　In Chinese, each syllable is an integral whole and corresponds to one Chinese character. And the Chinese words ai [ai] (to love) and mai [mai] (to buy) do not sound exactly like the English words *I* [ai] and *my* [mai]. (Please listen to the recording.)

2.　ai ei ao ou

In the compound finals ai, ei, ao and ou, the first vowels [a], [e], [a] and [o] are a bit prolonged and louder while the second vowels [i] and [u] are shorter and less distinct.

3.　[n] and [ŋ]

The end of the finals an and en is [n] while the end of the finals ang, eng and ong is [ŋ].

4.　Syllable-dividing mark '

The mark ' is used before syllables beginning with a, o, e when they might be joined incorrectly to syllables preceding them. Compare:

pí'ǎo	(*fur-lined jacket*, two syllables)
piāo	(*float*, one syllable)

轻声　Qīngshēng　**Neutral tone**

Some syllables are pronounced in a low and unstressed tone, known as the neutral tone (qīngshēng), which is shown by the absence of a tone mark, e.g.

nǐmen	you (plural form)
tāmen	they, them
bàba	father

māma   mother

tā de   his, her, its

Do the phonemes g, k, h exist in your native language? If so, please give an example. If not, try to find a similar one and explain their differences.

Read aloud the following words.

gàn to do	kàn to look	gǒu dog	kǒu mouth
gāo tall	hǎi sea	hóng red	lěng cold
hěn very	hǎo good	kāi to open	mén door
dōng east	dǒng to understand	děng to wait	dēng lamp
hēibǎn blackboard	bāngmáng lend a hand		
gēge elder brother	mèimei younger sister		

文化点   Wénhuà Diǎn   **Cultural notes**

The Chinese language has a long history. The oracle bone inscriptions (Chinese characters carved on tortoise shells and ox bones) appeared more than three thousand years ago. These writings were already a quite complex system. And of course the Chinese language existed long before its writing system evolved.

0.4

 会话 Huìhuà **Conversation**

A: Qǐng   wèn,
   please   ask
   Excuse me.
   zhèr yǒu   xǐshǒujiān   ma?
   here have wash-hand-room *a question particle*
   Is there a washroom here?

B: Yǒu.
   have
   Yes, there is.

A: Zài nǎr?
   be in/at where
   Where is it?

B: Zài   nàr.
   be in/at there
   It's over there.

* * * *

A: Qǐng   wèn,   xǐshǒujiān   zài   nǎr?
   please   ask   wash-hand-room   be in/at   where
   Excuse me, where is the washroom?

B: Wǎng   qián zǒu,   wǎng zuǒ guǎi.
   towards front go   towards left turn
   Go ahead, and turn left.

A: Shénme?
   What?

B: Wǎng   qián zǒu,   wǎng zuǒ guǎi.
   towards front go   towards left turn
   Go ahead, and turn left.

A: Xièxie.
   Thank you.

B: Bú kèqi.
   You are welcome.

* * * *

A: Wǒ yào qù yīyuàn.
   I   want go hospital
   I want to go to the hospital.

B: Hǎode.
   OK.

A: Qǐng kuài yìdiǎnr.
   Please fast a little
   Please be quick.

B: Méi   wèntí!

Not-have question/problem

No problem.

Activity

Role play (a): Ask the way.

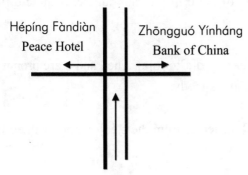

Hépíng Fàndiàn
Peace Hotel

Zhōngguó Yínháng
Bank of China

Words for reference:

qián	front, ahead	hòu	behind
zuǒ	left side	yòu	right side

Role play (b): Tell the taxi driver where you want to go.

Words for reference:

yīyuàn	hospital	fàndiàn	restaurant, hotel
bīnguǎn	guesthouse, hotel	jīchǎng	airport
huǒchēzhàn	railway station		

语音 Yǔyīn Phonetics

声母和韵母 Shēngmǔ hé Yùnmǔ Initials and finals

ya	ye	yao	you	yan	yin	yang	ying	yu	yue	yuan	yun	yong
(=ia	=ie	=iao	=iou	=ian	=in	=iang	=ing	=ü	=üe	=üan	=ün	=iong)
jia	jie	jiao	jiu	jian	jin	jiang	jing	ju	jue	juan	jun	jiong
			=jiou					=jü	=jüe	=jüan	=jün	
qia	qie	qiao	qiu	qian	qin	qiang	qing	qu	que	quan	qun	qiong
			=qiou					=qü	=qüe	=qüan	=qün	
xia	xie	xiao	xiu	xian	xin	xiang	xing	xu	xue	xuan	xun	xiong
			=xiou					=xü	=xüe	=xüan	=xün	

Notes:

1. ya ye yao you yan yin yang ying yu yue yuan yun yong

    When standing as syllables by themselves, ia, ie, iao, iou, ian, in, iang, ing, ü, üe, üan, ün, iong are written as ya, ye, yao, you, yan, yin, yang, ying, yu, yue, yuan, yun, yong.

2. iu

    When preceded by an initial, iou is written as iu, e.g. liu, jiu.

3. The omission of the two dots over ü

    When the final ü and other finals beginning with ü are preceded by the initials j, q or x, the two dots over ü are omitted, e.g. qu, jun, xue. Therefore, the sound of the u in du, diu, jiu, etc. is quite different from the u in ju, jue, qun, etc.

4. ia ie üe

    The ia, ie, üe are produced by gliding quickly from i or ü to a[a] or e[ɛ]. The i and ü are pronounced lightly while a [a] and e [ɛ] should be pronounced loudly and distinctly.

5. ie üe ian üan

    The e and a in the ie, üe, ian, üan are pronounced [ɛ], different from the e [ə] in eng or the a [a] in ang.

6. j q x

    Don't pronounce j [tɕ], q [tɕ'], x [ɕ] the same as [tʃ], [tʃ'], [ʃ]. (see picture)

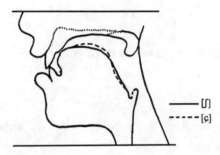

----------- [ʃ]

- - - - - - [ɕ]

第三声的变调   Dì-sān Shēng De Biàndiào   3ᵗʰ tone sandhi

The 3ʳᵈ tone is seldom used in full except in independent syllables or when followed by a long pause.

When a 3ʳᵈ tone is followed by another 3ʳᵈ tone, the first one changes into a second tone. For example, nǐ hǎo, hěn xiǎo sound almost the same as ní hǎo, hén xiǎo.

When a 3ʳᵈ tone is followed by 1ˢᵗ tone, 2ⁿᵈ tone or 4ᵗʰ tone, it retains the first falling part, but drops almost all of the rising part.

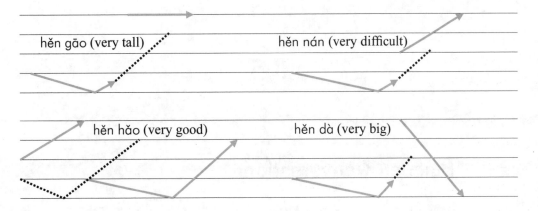

hěn gāo (very tall)   hěn nán (very difficult)

hěn hǎo (very good)   hěn dà (very big)

Compare:

hěn hǎo   very good
      (hěn is pronounced in a rising tone, like the 2nd tone)

hěn gāo   very tall
      (hěn is pronounced in a low-falling tone)

Do the phonemes j, q, x exist in your native language? If so, please give an example. If not, try to find a similar one and explain their differences.

Read aloud the following words.

jiā home
qián money
xiǎo small, little
yún cloud
xuéxí to study, to learn
niúnǎi milk
tàiyáng the sun
kànjiàn to see
Yīngyǔ the English language
hěn hǎo very good
hěn dà very big
lǎobǎn boss
lǎowài foreigner

jiào to call
qù to go
xiě to write
yuè month
xiūxi have a rest
xióngmāo panda

jiǔ alcoholic drink
qǐng please
xiǎng to think
yuǎn far

yuèliang the moon
yínháng bank
yīnyuè music
hěn duō quite a few
hěn máng very busy
lǎojiā old home; native place
lǎorén old people

0.5

A: Zhè　ge　　jiào shénme?
　　this *measure word* call　what
　　What do you call this (in Chinese)?

B: Píngguǒ.
　　Apple.

A: Nà　ge　　jiào　shénme?
　　that *measure word* call　　what
　　What do you call that (in Chinese)?

B: Xiāngjiāo. Nǐ　yào bu yào?

banana   you want not want
Banana. Do you want (to buy)?

A: Wǒ bú yào.
I not want
No.

* * *

A: Nǐ   yào shénme?
You want what
What do you want?

B: Wǒ yào zhè ge.
I   want this *measure word*
I want (to buy) this.

B: Nǐ   yào   jǐ   ge ?
you want how many *measure word*
How many do you want (to buy)?

A: Wǒ yào wǔ ge.   Duōshao   qián?
I want five *measure word*   how many/much   money
I want to buy five.   How much is it?

B: Qī   kuài wǔ máo.
seven *kuai* five *mao*
Seven yuan and fifty cents.

* * *

A: Zhè ge   duōshao   qián?
this *measure word* how many/much   money
How much is it?

B: Jiǔshísì kuài.   Yào   ma?
nine-ten four *kuai*   want *a question particle*
Ninety-four yuan.   Do you want it?

A: ......

B: Yào ma?
Do you want it?

A: ......

B: Yào bu yào?
want not want
Do you want it?

A: Tài guì le! Bú yào. Zàijiàn!
too expensive *a particle* not want again see
It's too expensive. I don't want it. Goodbye.

Activity

Role play: Go shopping.

Words for reference:

hǎo	good
piàoliang	beautiful
guì	expensive
Tài guì le.	It's so/too expensive.
piányi	cheap
Néng bu néng piányi yìdiǎnr?	Can it be a bit cheaper?

 ## 语音 Yǔyīn **Phonetics**

声母和韵母 Shēngmǔ hé Yùnmǔ **Initials and finals**

	wu	wa	wo	wai	wei	wan	wen	wang	weng
	(=u	=ua	=uo	=uai	=uei	=uan	=uen	=uang	=ueng)
zi	zu		zuo		zui	zuan	zun		
					=zuei		=zuen		
ci	cu		cuo		cui	cuan	cun		
					=cuei		=cuen		
si	su		suo		sui	suan	sun		
					=suei		=suen		

Notes:

1. wu wa wo wai wei wan wen wang

   Standing as syllables by themselves, u, ua, uo, uai, uei, uan, uen and uang should be written as wu, wa, wo, wai, wei, wan, wen and wang.

2. ui un

   When preceded by an initial, uei and uen are written as ui and un, e.g. zui, dun.

3. ua uo

   In the syllables ua and uo, a [a] and o [o] are louder and more distinct than u.

4. z c

   The initial z sounds like the *ds* in *reads* (but de-voiced), c sounds the same as *ts* in *boots*.

5. zi ci si

   The final i in zi, ci and si is pronounced as [ɿ], not [i]. The vowel [i] never follows z, c and s in Putonghua.

Do the phonemes z, c, s exist in your native language? If so, please give an example. If not, try to find a similar one and explain their differences.

Read aloud the following words.

wǒ I, me	huǒ fire	cuò wrong
cài dish	huài bad	kuài fast
duì correct	huì can	kùn sleepy
guān to close	duǎn short	huáng yellow
zìjǐ oneself	zàijiàn goodbye	zǎofàn breakfast
cōngming clever	cānguān to visit	cídiǎn dictionary
sījī driver	sēnlín forest	suānnǎi yoghurt
gōngzuò work, job	cèsuǒ toilet	wèikǒu appetite
wénhuà culture	zuǐba mouth	sūnzi grandson

文化点 Wénhuà Diǎn **Cultural notes**

Although the language we call Chinese probably existed well over ten thousand years ago, the name "Hànyǔ" referring to the Chinese language came about rather late. Prior to the Qin Dynasty (221 BC-206 BC), the Chinese called themselves "Huá" or "Xià." During the Han Dynasty (206 BC-220 AD), other nations referred to the Chinese as the "Han people". Such names as the "Han people", the "Qin people", and the "Tang people" all came about because these were the names of ruling dynasties during different historical times. Hence, at the present time, the "language of the Han people" is best called "Hànyǔ".

The reason that the "Han Dynasty" was so named is because its first Emperor, Liu Bang (256 BC-195 BC), was called the King of Han. The reason he was called the King of Han is that he was enfeoffed in the middle reaches of the Han River (Hàn Shuǐ, also known as Hàn Jiāng).

0.6

A: Jīntiān xīngqī   jǐ?
   today   week   how many/how much
   What day is today?

                [zuótiān   míngtiān]
                yesterday   tomorrow

B: Jīntiān xīngqīyī.
   today week one
   Today is Monday.

   [Xīngqī'èr   Xīngqīsān   Xīngqīsì   Xīngqīwǔ   Xīngqīliù   Xīngqītiān (Xīngqīrì)]
     Tuesday   Wednesday Thursday   Friday   Saturday   Sunday

                        *   *   *

A: Nǐ jīntiān yǒu kè   ma ?
   you today have class *a question particle*

Do you have classes today?

B: Jīntiān shàngwǔ yǒu kè,   xiàwǔ   méiyǒu   kè.
today   morning have classes afternoon not-have classes
I have classes this morning. I don't have classes this afternoon.

Nǐ   ne?
you *a particle*
What about you?

A: Wǒ shàngbān.
I   go to work
I'll go to work.

*   *   *

A: Wǎnshang gàn shénme?
evening   do what
What will you do this evening?

B: Kàn shū.   Nǐmen   ne?
look book   you (plural form) *a particle*
I'll do some reading. What about you?

C: Wǒ kàn   diànshì.
I   look/watch TV
I'll watch TV.

A: Wǒ shàngwǎng.
I   get on   net
I'll surf the Internet.

Activity

Role play: Ask each other's plan for today.

Words for reference:

shàngkè	go to class; attend class
shàngbān	go to work
shàngwǎng	surf the Internet; be on the Internet
kàn diànshì	watch TV
kàn shū	read (a book)

dǎ qiú   *play sport*

语音 Yǔyīn **Phonetics**

声母和韵母 Shēngmǔ hé Yùnmǔ **Initials and finals**

zhi chi shi ri
er

Notes:

zhi chi shi ri

The final in zhi, chi, shi and ri is pronounced [ʅ], not [i]. The vowel [i] never follows zh, ch, sh and r in Putonghua.

Zhi, chi, shi are pronounced almost the same way as zi, ci, si except that the tip of the tongue is raised towards the hard palate. (see picture)

zh ch sh

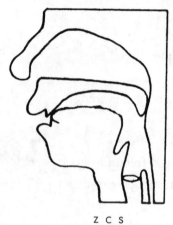

z c s

儿化韵 Érhuà Yùn **Retroflex final**

The final er is sometimes attached to another final to form a retroflex final and when thus used, it is no longer an independent syllable. A retroflex final is represented by the letter r added to the final, e.g.

zhèr here　　　nàr there　　　nǎr where

Do the phonemes zh, ch, sh, r exist in your native language? If so, please give an example. If not, try to find a similar one and explain their differences.

Read aloud the following words.

zhǎo look for
zhēnde true; really
chī to eat
chuānghu window
shū book

zhàn to stand
zhuōzi desk, table
chuān put on; to wear
qìchē automobile
shuǐ water

zhōng clock

chuán boat

shān mountain, hill

shāngdiàn store

rè hot

Rìběnrén Japanese

zhèr here

huār flower

xǐ shǒu wash hands

ruǎn soft

zhūròu pork

nàr there

wánr to play; have fun

ràng to let

rúguǒ if

nǎr where

0.7

A: Jīntiān   jǐ   hào ?

today   which   day/date

What's the date today?

B: Jīntiān shí'èr yuè   èrshíwǔ   hào.

today twelve month two-ten five day/date

Today is December 25th.

Jan	*Feb*	*Mar*	*April*	*May*	*June*
yī yuè	èr yuè	sān yuè	sì yuè	wǔ yuè	liù yuè
qī yuè	bā yuè	jiǔ yuè	shí yuè	shíyī yuè	shí'èr yuè
July	*August*	*sep*	*oct*	*nov*	*dem*

yī hào	èr hào	...	jiǔ hào	shí hào
shíyī hào	shí'èr hào	...	shíjiǔ hào	èrshí hào
èrshíyī hào	èrshí'èr hào	...	èrshíjiǔ hào	sānshí hào
sānshíyī hào				

*   *   *

A: Jīntiān tiānqì búcuò.

today weather not bad

It's fine today.

B: Shì a,   bù lěng bú rè,   hěn shūfu.

yes *a particle* not cold not hot very comfortable

Yes. It's neither cold nor hot. It's fine.

A: Zhè   zhī   xiǎo   gǒu hěn kě'ài.

this *mesure word* small/little dog very lovely

This little dog is very cute.

B: Xièxie!

Thank you!

*   *   *

A: Nǐmen   jīntiān gōngzuò bu gōngzuò?

you (plural form) today work not work

Do you work today?

B: Wǒ gōngzuò. Tā   bù gōngzuò, Tā   jīntiān xiūxi.

I   work he/she not work   he/she today rest

I work today. He/She doesn't work today. He/She has the day off.

Nǐ   hěn máng   ba?

you very busy *a particle*

(I think) you are quite busy?

A: Hái   kěyǐ.

passable, not bad

It's OK.

Activity

Role play: Exchange greetings.

Words for reference:

piàoliang   beautiful, pretty

kě'ài   lovely

shūfu   comfortable

búcuò	not bad; good
máng	busy
hái kěyǐ	passable; not bad

 ## 语音复习　Yǔyīn fūxí　**Phonetics revision**

声母　Shēngmǔ　**Initials**

b	p	m	f	d	t	n	l
g	k	h		j	q	x	
zh	ch	sh	r	z		c	s

韵母　Yùnmǔ　**Finals**

a	o	e	ai	ei	ao	ou	an	en	ang	eng	ong
i	ia		ie		iao	iou	ian	in	iang	ing	iong
u	ua	uo	uai	uei			uan	uen	uang	ueng	
ü		üe					üan	ün			
-i
er

声调　Shēngdiào　**Tones**

mā　má　mǎ　mà

轻声　Qīngshēng　**Neutral tone**

māma　mother

第三声的变调　Dì-sān Shēng De Biàndiào　**3rd tone sandhi**

shǒubiǎo	watch (n.)		
shǔbiāo	computer mouse	yǔyán	language
yǐnliào	soft drinks	ěrduo	ear

儿化韵 Érhuà Yùn **Retroflex final**

huār   flower   wánr   to play

The following words have been listed in 0.1. Read them again and ask your teacher to listen and point out what are your progress and problems.

dùzi	tùzi	shuìjiào	shuǐjiǎo	qǐngwèn	qīnwěn
zǐdàn	jīdàn	shǎoshù	xiǎoshù	zìjǐ	cíqì
yóuyù	měinǔ	fǎlù	xuéxí	xuǎnjǔ	chūqù
pángbiān	pànbié	shàng chuán	xióngzhuàng	jiāngjūn	
zhèngzhì	jīngjì	cānguān	kuānkuò	jiéhūn	
niúròu	shēngrì	rè'ài	chàng gē	zhèr	wǒmen

文化点   Wénhuà Diǎn   **Cultural notes**

Hanyu, the Chinese language, includes the following dialect groups: (1) The mandarin or Putonghua (literally, common speech) dialect group, used by more than 70% of all Han Chinese, the best known form of which is the Beijing dialect; (2) Wú dialects, represented by Shanghainese; (3) Xiāng dialects, including many forms spoken in Húnán Province; (4) Gàn dialects, used in Jiāngxī Province; (5) Hakka (Kèjiā) dialects, represented by speech found in Méi County (Méi Xiàn) in Guǎngdōng Province but found throughout Guǎngdōng, Guǎngxī, Fújiàn, Jiāngxī and other places; (6) Mǐn dialects, which are distributed throughout Fújiàn Province, Cháozhōu and Shàntóu districts of Guǎngdōng Province, Hǎinán Province, and most of Táiwān; and (7) Yuè dialects, also known as Cantonese. The differences between dialects lie mainly in the pronunciation, certain vocabulary items and to a certain extent, grammar. They can differ as widely from each other as French and Italian.

Unit 1

Nǐ Hǎo！
你 好！
Hello!

Learning objectives

* Identifying one's name
* Identifying one's nationality
* Identifying one's language

Key sentences

Nín guìxìng?
您 贵姓?
What's your surname?

Nǐ jiào shénme míngzi?
你叫 什么 名字?
What's your name?

Nǐ shuō Yīngyǔ háishi shuō Fǎyǔ?
你说 英语 还是 说 法语?
Do you speak English or French?

1.1

Nǐ Jiào Shénme Míngzi ?

你 叫 什么 名字 ?

What's your name?

Preliminary exercises

1 Warm up

Recall the sentences you learned in Unit 0: How to ask a person's name? How to ask a person's nationality?

2 Learn the following words and form correct sentences with the words under the teacher's guidance.

（1）好 你

（2）什么 叫 你 名字

（3）哪 人 国 他 是

（4）加拿大 我 人 是

（5）中国 她 人 是 不

3 Learn the following words and choose the correct answer to fill in the blanks according to the recording.

什么 哪 吗 呢 也 不

（1）你叫 _____ 名字？

（2）你是 _____ 国人？

（3）我是加拿大人，你 _____ ？

（4）你们是中国人 _____ ？

（5）他是中国人，我 _____ 是中国人，我是加拿大人。

（6）我们 _____ 是中国人，我们是澳大利亚人。

Questions:

Should the question words in Chinese be put at the beginning of the sentences?

What do 也 and 不 mean? Where do they usually be put in a sentence?

Do 吗 and 呢 have the same usage? When should we use 吗? When should we use 呢?

3 （1）你叫什么名字？（2）你是哪国人？（3）我是加拿大人，你呢？（4）你们是中国人吗？（5）他是中国人，我也是中国人，我是加拿大人。（6）我们不是中国人，我们是澳大利亚人。

Listening script

⬇ Words and expressions

1.	我	(Pron.)	wǒ	I, me
2.	你	(Pron.)	nǐ	you
3.	他	(Pron.)	tā	he, him
4.	她	(Pron.)	tā	she, her
5.	们	(suffix for plural form)	men	used after a personal pronoun or a noun to show plural form
6.	叫	(V.)	jiào	call
7.	什么	(QW)	shénme	what
8.	名字	(N.)	míngzi	name
9.	好	(Adj.)	hǎo	good, well, fine
10.	是	(V.)	shì	be
11.	哪国人		nǎ guó rén	what nationality
	哪	(QW)	nǎ	which
	国		guó	country
	人	(N.)	rén	people, person
12.	不	(Adv.)	bù	no, not
13.	也	(Adv.)	yě	also, too
14.	吗	(Part.)	ma	used at the end of interrogatwe sentence
15.	呢	(Part.)	ne	marker of a special, alternative or rhetorical question

Proper nouns

1.	加拿大	Jiānádà	Canada
2.	澳大利亚	Àodàlìyà	Australia
3.	中国	Zhōngguó	China

⚙ Listen to the dialogue and answer the following questions. (Try best to answer in Chinese.)

（1）How many people are there in the recording?

（2）What are their names?

（3）Where are they from?

⚙ Listen to the recording while reading the text on the right. ⇨

⚙ Read aloud the text and try not to look at the pinyin.

⚙ Work in groups and act out the conversation.

⚙ Activity: Ask the names and nationalities of the people in your group.

	姓名 xìngmíng Name	国籍 guójí Nationality		姓名 xìngmíng Name	国籍 guójí Nationality
1			4		
2			5		
3			6		

⚙ Introduce yourself to your classmates and write down what you have said.

_____

_____

_____

_____

Vocabulary extension

英国	Yīngguó	the United Kingdom	俄罗斯	Éluósī	Russia
法国	Fǎguó	France	德国	Déguó	Germany
日本	Rìběn	Japan	韩国	Hánguó	South Korea
亚洲	Yàzhōu	Asia	欧洲	Ōuzhōu	Europe
美洲	Měizhōu	America	大洋洲	Dàyángzhōu	Oceania
非洲	Fēizhōu	Africa			
华裔	huáyì	foreign citizen of Chinese origin			

Text

Bai Xiaohong, a girl from China, Wang Ying, a Canadian girl of Chinese ancestry, and Martin, a man from Australia, study in the same university. This is their first meeting.

Bái Xiǎohóng: Nǐmen hǎo !
白小红：你们好！

Wáng Yīng: Nǐ hǎo !
王 英：你好！

Mǎdīng: Nǐ hǎo !
马 丁：你好！

Wáng Yīng: Nǐ jiào shénme míngzi ?
王 英：(to Bai Xiaohong) 你叫 什么 名字？

> **"名字 míngzi"** can either refer to one's given name or the whole name.

Bái Xiǎohóng: Wǒ jiào Bái Xiǎohóng. Nǐmen ne ?
白小红：我叫 白 小 红。你们 呢？

Wáng Yīng: Wǒ jiào Wáng Yīng.
王 英：我叫 王 英。

Mǎdīng: Wǒ jiào Mǎdīng.
马 丁：我叫 马丁。

Wáng Yīng: Nǐ shì nǎ guó rén ?
王 英：(to Bai Xiaohong) 你是 哪国人？

> **"哪国人 nǎ guó rén"** is used in a spoken style. The formal written form for nationality is **"国籍 guójí"**.

Bái Xiǎohóng: Wǒ shì Zhōngguórén. Nǐ ne?
白小红：我是 中国人。你呢？

Wáng Yīng: Wǒ shì Jiānádàrén.
王 英：我是 加拿大人。

Bái Xiǎohóng: Nǐ yě shì Jiānádàrén ma?
白小红：(to Martin) 你也是 加拿大人吗？

Mǎdīng: Bù, wǒ bú shì Jiānádàrén , wǒ shì Àodàlìyàrén.
马 丁：不，我不是 加拿大人，我是 澳大利亚人。

1.2

Nín Guìxìng?

您 贵姓？

What's your surname?

Preliminary exercises

1 Warm up

Do you know any Chinese surnames?

Can you say the names of several famous Chinese people?

2 Learn the following words and form correct sentences with the words under the teacher's guidance.

（1）您 贵 姓

（2）我 马 姓 不

（3）老师 张 是 他

（4）他们 美国人 是 都

（5）同学们 汉语 说 只

（6）英语 法语 还是 说 你们

3 Learn the following words and choose the correct answer to fill in the blanks according to the recording.

都 只 不 还是

（1）你是 _____ 是中国人？

（2）你说 _____ 说汉语？

（3）你是美国人 _____ 英国人？

（4）你说英语 _____ 法语？

（5）我们 _____ 说汉语。

（6）他 _____ 说英语。

Questions:

Should an interrogative sentence in Chinese always end with the question word 吗？

Are there other ways to ask Sentences 1 and 2? Can 吗 be used?

What do 都 and 只 mean? Where are they usually placed in a sentence?

Words and expressions

1.	您贵姓		nín guìxìng	What's your surname?
2.	您	(Pron.)	nín	you (honorific form)
3.	姓	(V. & N.)	xìng	surname
4.	同学	(N.)	tóngxué	classmate
5.	老师	(N.)	lǎoshī	teacher
6.	说	(V.)	shuō	say, speak
7.	汉语	(N.)	Hànyǔ	Chinese (language)
8.	英语	(N.)	Yīngyǔ	English (language)
9.	法语	(N.)	Fǎyǔ	French (language)
10.	还是	(Conj.)	háishi	or
11.	都	(Adv.)	dōu	both, all
12.	只	(Adv.)	zhǐ	only

Proper nouns

1.	美国	Měiguó	the United States
2.	英国	Yīngguó	the United Kingdom

⚙ Listen to the dialogue and answer the following questions. (Try best to answer in Chinese.)

（1）How many people are there in the recording?

（2）What are their names? Where are they from?

（3）Do the students speak English? What about Mr. Zhang?

⚙ Listen to the recording while reading the text on the right. ⇨

⚙ Read aloud the text and try not to look at the pinyin.

⚙ Work in groups and act out the conversation.

⚙ Activity: Use the following words to ask each other's nationalities and languages one can speak.

是不是　还是　说不说

Vocabulary extension

中文	Zhōngwén	Chinese language	
普通话	Pǔtōnghuà	Mandarin (Putonghua; Common Speech)	
英文	Yīngwén	English language	
法文	Fǎwén	French language	
西班牙语 / 西班牙文	Xībānyáyǔ / Xībānyáwén	Spanish language	
葡萄牙语 / 葡萄牙文	Pútáoyáyǔ / Pútáoyáwén	Portuguese language	
俄语 / 俄文	Éyǔ / Éwén	Russian language	
德语 / 德文	Déyǔ / Déwén	German language	
日语 / 日文	Rìyǔ / Rìwén	Japanese language	
韩语 / 韩文	Hányǔ / Hánwén	Korean language	

Text

Martin, Wang Ying and Jiang Shan have just started to learn Chinese. Zhang Lin is their Chinese teacher.

Tóngxuémen:　Lǎoshī hǎo!
同学们：老师好!

Zhāng lǎoshī:　Tóngxuémen hǎo!
张老师：同学们 好!

> Here "同学 tóngxué" is used as a form of address when the teacher speaks to students.

Mǎdīng:　Lǎoshī,　Nín guìxìng?
马 丁：老师，您贵姓?

Zhāng lǎoshī:　Wǒ xìng Zhāng, jiào Zhāng Lín.　Nǐ jiào shénme míngzi?
张老师：我姓 张，叫 张 林。你叫 什么 名字?

Mǎdīng:　Wǒ jiào Mǎdīng.
马 丁：我叫 马 丁。

> "您贵姓" nín guìxìng" is a polite form to ask for the family name of the elders or strangers.

Zhāng lǎoshī:　Nǐ shì nǎ guó rén?
张老师：你是 哪国人?

Mǎdīng:　Wǒ shì Àodàlìyàrén.
马 丁：我是 澳大利亚人。

Zhāng lǎoshī:　Nǐ ne?
张老师：(to Jiang Shan)你呢?

Jiāng Shān:　Wǒ jiào Jiāng Shān, shì Měiguórén.
江 山：我叫 江 山，是 美国人。

Zhāng lǎoshī:　Nǐ yě shì Měiguórén ma?
张老师：(to Wang Ying)你也是 美国人 吗?

Wáng Yīng:　Bù, wǒ bú shì Měiguórén.　Wǒ shì Jiānádàrén.
王 英：不，我不是 美国人。我是 加拿大人。

Zhāng lǎoshī:　Nǐ shuō Yīngyǔ háishi shuō Fǎyǔ?
张老师：你说 英语还是 说法语?

Wáng Yīng:　Wǒ shuō Yīngyǔ.　Wǒmen dōu shuō Yīngyǔ.　Zhāng lǎoshī, nín
王 英：我说 英语。我们 都 说 英语。张老师，您

shuō bu shuō Yīngyǔ?
说 不说 英语?

> Students usually address their teachers by "surname + laoshi".

Zhāng lǎoshī:　Wǒ bù shuō Yīngyǔ.　Wǒ zhǐ shuō Hànyǔ.
张老师：我不说 英语。我只说 汉语。

1.3 Language Points

❖ Tone changes for 不

"不 bù", is usually pronounced in the fourth tone, e.g.

bù + 1st tone	e.g. 不说汉语 bù shuō Hànyǔ	not speak Chinese
bù + 2nd tone	e.g. 不白 bù bái	not white
bù + 3rd tone	e.g. 不好 bù hǎo	not good

bú + 4th tone

But when put before another 4th tone syllable, "不 bù" changes into the 2nd tone.

(1) 我不是中国人。 Wǒ bú shì Zhōngguórén. I am not Chinese.

(2) 我不姓王。 Wǒ bú xìng Wáng. My surname is not Wang.

❖ In Chinese, grammatical relationships are shown either by word order or function words such as prepositions and particles, rather than by affixes or changes in the word itself, though modern Chinese has developed a very small number of quasi-sufixes which function as grammatical determinatives. Compare:

我是老师。	Wǒ shì lǎoshī.	I am a teacher.
他是老师。	Tā shì lǎoshī.	He is a teacher.
我们都是老师。	Wǒmen dōu shì lǎoshī.	We are all teachers.

❖ Simple sentence pattern 1: Subject + Verb (+ Object)

Just like English, the Chinese simple sentence pattern is:

Subject + Verb (+ Object)

the affirmative form

我姓王。
Wǒ xìng Wáng.

我说英语。
Wǒ shuō Yīngyǔ.

the negative form

我不姓王。 *I Not surname Wáng*
Wǒ bú xìng Wáng.

我不说英语。
Wǒ bù shuō Yīngyǔ. *I Not talk english*

我们都是中国人。　　　　我们都不是中国人。
Wǒmen dōu shì Zhōngguórén. Wǒmen dōu bú shì Zhōngguórén. *none of us is chinese*

But unlike English, the Chinese adverb is always put before the verb, not after it.

Adverb + Verb

他不是美国人。
Tā bú shì Měiguórén.

他也是美国人。
Tā yě shì Měiguórén.

他们都是美国人。
Tāmen dōu shì Měiguórén.

他只说汉语。
Tā zhǐ shuō Hànyǔ.

❦ Question patterns

In Chinese, word order in questions is the same as in statements. The most commonly used types of questions are as follows:

A. Questions with " 吗 ma", which are yes-or-no questions.

a statement + 吗?

（1）您是中国人吗?
　　　Nín shì Zhōngguórén ma?　　Are you a Chinese?

（2）他也是中国人吗?
　　　Tā yě shì Zhōngguórén ma?　Is he a Chinese too?

（3）你们都说汉语吗?
　　　Nǐmen dōu shuō Hànyǔ ma?　Do you all speak Chinese?

B. Choice questions, which include two sub-types:

a.

X 不 X ...?

Here "不 bu", is pronounced in the neutral tone.

（1）您是不是中国人？

Nín shì bu shì Zhōngguórén? Are you a Chinese?

（2）他是不是中国人？

Tā shì bu shì Zhōngguórén?   Is he a Chinese?

（3）你们说不说汉语？

Nǐmen shuō bu shuō Hànyǔ?   Do you speak Chinese?

Note: the *X 不 bu X* pattern means almost the same as the "*...吗 ma*" pattern. But in the *X 不 bu X* pattern, the verb cannot be modified by such adverbs as 也 , 都 or 只 .

b.

X 还是 Y？

（1）你是加拿大人还是美国人？

Nǐ shì Jiānádàrén háishi Měiguórén?

Are you Canadian or American?

（2）你说英语还是（说）法语？

Nǐ shuō Yīngyǔ háishi (shuō) Fǎyǔ.

Do you speak English or French?

c.

Questions with a question word

（1）你是哪国人？

Nǐ shì nǎ guó rén?

What's your nationality?

（2）你姓什么？

Nǐ xìng shénme?

What's your surname?

（3）你叫什么名字？

Nǐ jiào shénme míngzi?

What's your name?

D. Questions of shortened form ending with "呢 ne", meaning "how about/what about…".

NP. + 呢？

（1）A: 您是中国人吗？　　　　　Nín shì Zhōngguórén ma?

　　　B: 我是中国人。你呢？　　　Wǒ shì Zhōngguórén. Nǐ ne?

　　　A: 我是加拿大人。　　　　　Wǒ shì Jiānádàrén.

（2）A: 你叫什么名字？　　　　　Nǐ jiào shénme míngzi?

　　　B: 我叫江山。你呢？　　　　Wǒ jiào Jiāng Shān. Nǐ ne?

　　　A: 我叫白小红。　　　　　　Wǒ jiào Bái Xiǎohóng.

（3）A: 你说英语还是说法语？　　Nǐ shuō Yīngyǔ háishi shuō Fǎyǔ?

　　　B: 我说英语。你呢？　　　　Wǒ shuō Yīngyǔ. Nǐ ne?

　　　A: 我也说英语。　　　　　　Wǒ yě shuō Yīngyǔ.

❀ Review exercises: Choose the correct sentences.

（1）A. 我不说汉语。　　　　　　　　　（2）　A. 什么名字你叫？
　　　B. 我汉语说不。　　　　　　　　　　　　B. 你什么名字叫？
　　　C. 我说汉语不。　　　　　　　　　　　　C. 你叫什么名字？

（3）A. 我们说汉语都。　　　　　　　　　（4）　A. 我是加拿大人，你呢？
　　　B. 我们都说汉语。　*all of us*　　　　　　B. 我是加拿大人，你吗？
　　　C. 都我们说汉语。　*speak english*　　　　C. 我是加拿大人，你什么？

（5）A. 你是不是英国人？　　　　　　　（6）　A. 你说英语还是法语吗？
　　　B. 你是不是英国人吗？　　　　　　　　　B. 英语还是法语你说吗？
　　　C. 你是不是也英国人？　　　　　　　　　C. 你说英语还是法语？

文化点　Wénhuà Diǎn　Cultural notes

❀ A complete Chinese name consists of a surname (xìng) and a given name (míng), the former preceding the latter. Surnames are usually monosyllabic/one character, but a few surnames are disyllabic/two characters. Given names may be either monosyllabic or disyllabic.

姓名 xìngmíng Full Name	姓 xìng Surname	名 míng Given Name
白小红 Bái Xiǎohóng	白 Bái	小红 Xiǎohóng
张 林 Zhāng Lín	张 Zhāng	林 Lín

❀ When asking someone's name, we say, "Nǐ jiào shénme míngzi? (What is your name?)"; "Nín guìxìng? (What is your honourable surname?)"; or "Nín zěnme chēnghu? (How do I address you?)" The last two are more polite expressions.

❀ Modern Chinese may be broadly or narrowly defined. In its broader definition, it includes all the dialects. In its narrower interpretation, it refers to Chinese with a pronunciation based on the Beijing dialect and grammar based on the model of modern vernacular writings. It is commonly called Mandarin or Putonghua.

❀ The terms "Zhōngwén", "Hànyǔ", "Guóyǔ" and "Huáyǔ" are similar in meaning. "Guóyǔ" is used to refer to "Mandarin" in regions like Taiwan, while "Huáyǔ" is used in Singapore and among many overseas Chinese.

Madarin: Pǔtōnghùa/han yǔ/zhōng wén

Unit 2

Hěn Gāoxìng Rènshi Nín !
很 高兴 认识 您!
Glad to Meet You!

Learning objectives

* Exchanging personal information
* Making comments
* Receiving guests

Key sentences

Hěn gāoxìng rènshi nín!
很 高兴 认识 您!
Glad to meet you!

Wǒ zài jìn-chūkǒu gōngsī gōngzuò.
我 在 进出口 公司 工作。
I work in an import and export corporation.

Qǐng zuò, qǐng hē chá!
请 坐, 请 喝 茶!
Sit down please, and have a cup of tea.

Dōngfāng Xuéyuàn zěnmeyàng?
东方 学院 怎么样?
What is Eastern College like?

Dōngfāng Xuéyuàn hěn dà, yě hěn piàoliang.
东方 学院 很 大, 也 很 漂亮。
Eastern College is big, and is also beautiful.

2.1

Wǒ Zài Jìn-chūkǒu Gōngsī Gōngzuò

我 在 进出口 公司 工作

I work in an import and export corporation

Preliminary exercises

1 Warm up

Are you at work or at school? How do you say it in Chinese?

Recall how to say 1 to 10 in Chinese, which you learned in Unit 0. Say several numbers and ask your classmate to write them down.

2 Read aloud the following telephone numbers.

9758104   33041218   13817194562   86-21-65642222

3 Learn the following words and form correct sentences with the words under the teacher's guidance.

（1）高兴 我 认识 您 很

（2）我 工作 进出口 公司 在

（3）合作 可以 我们

（4）你 可以 发 电子邮件 给我

（5）我 可以 可以 不 打电话 给你

4 Learn the following words and choose the correct answer to fill in the blanks according to the recording.

给 在 的

（1）你 _____ 汉语很好。

（2）我 _____ 杰克 _____ 公司工作。

（3）你可以 _____ 我打电话，也可以 _____ 我发电子邮件。

Questions:

What does 的 mean in Chinese?

Should the prepositional phrases 在… and 给… be put before or after a verb?

Words and expressions

1.	很	(Adv.)	hěn	very
2.	高兴	(Adj.)	gāoxìng	glad
3.	认识	(V.)	rènshi	know
4.	谢谢	(V.)	xièxie	thank
5.	在	(Prep. & V.)	zài	(be) in, at
6.	进出口		jìn-chūkǒu	import and export
	进口	(V.)	jìnkǒu	import
	出口	(V.)	chūkǒu	export
7.	公司	(N.)	gōngsī	company
8.	工作	(V. & N.)	gōngzuò	work; job
9.	可以	(M. V.)	kěyǐ	may, can
10.	合作	(V.)	hézuò	cooperate
11.	给……打电话		gěi … dǎ diànhuà	call sb.
	给	(Prep.)	gěi	to, for
	电话	(N.)	diànhuà	telephone
12.	号码	(N.)	hàomǎ	number
13.	○（零）	(Num.)	líng	zero
14.	发	(V.)	fā	send
15.	电子邮件		diànzǐ yóujiàn	email
	电子	(N.)	diànzǐ	electronic
	邮件	(N.)	yóujiàn	mail
16.	的	(Part.)	de	我的 my, mine 我们的 our, ours
17.	是的		shì de	yes
18.	好的		hǎo de	OK; all right

Unit
2

⚙ Listen to the dialogue and answer the following questions. (Try best to answer in Chinese.)

（1）Do Ding Hansheng and Jack work in the same company?

（2）What are they planning to do?

（3）Will Jack call Ding Hansheng or send him an email?

⚙ Listen to the recording while reading the text on the right. ⇨

⚙ Read aloud the text and try not to look at the pinyin.

⚙ Work in groups and act out the conversation.

⚙ Activity: Role play the following people. Work in pairs and get to know each other.

王一天：大学教授	林　克：公司经理
张　红：医生	江中月：学生

⚙ Make a name card for yourself using the following model.

中国进出口公司

江　林　经理

地址：北京大同路 310 号　　电话：010-65678931

电子邮箱：jianglin@hotmail.com

Vocabulary extension

职员	zhíyuán	employee	医生	yīshēng	doctor
工程师	gōngchéngshī	engineer	经理	jīnglǐ	manager
服务员	fúwùyuán	waiter, waitress	律师	lǜshī	lawyer
教授	jiàoshòu	professor	名片	míngpiàn	name card
邮箱	yóuxiāng	mail box	地址	dìzhǐ	address

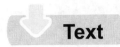

Text

Jack is the manager of a local import and export company. Ding Hansheng is the head of the overseas branch of a Chinese import and export company. They are meeting at a large trade fair.

Jiékè:　　　Nín hǎo !
杰　克：　您好！

Dīng Hànshēng:　Nín hǎo !
丁　汉生：　您好！

Jiékè:　　　Wǒ zài jìn-chūkǒu gōngsī gōngzuò.
杰　克：　我在进出口 公司工作。

Dīng Hànshēng:　Wǒ yě zài jìn-chūkǒu gōngsī gōngzuò.
丁　汉生：　我也在进出口公司工作。（exchanging name cards）

Jiékè:　　　Hěn gāoxìng rènshi nín !
杰　克：　很高兴认识您！

> "（我）很高兴认识您" or "认识您（我）很高兴" is a formal way to greet people.

Dīng Hànshēng:　Wǒ yě hěn gāoxìng !　Nín de Hànyǔ hěn hǎo !
丁　汉生：　我也很高兴！您的汉语很好！

Jiékè:　　　Xièxie !　Wǒmen dōu zài jìn-chūkǒu gōngsī gōngzuò …
杰　克：　谢谢！我们 都在进出口公司工作……

Dīng Hànshēng:　Wǒmen kěyǐ hézuò.
丁　汉生：　我们可以合作。

Jiékè:　　　Shì de , kěyǐ hézuò.
杰　克：　是的，可以合作。

Dīng Hànshēng:　Nín kěyǐ gěi wǒ dǎ diànhuà , yě kěyǐ gěi wǒ fā diànzǐ yóujiàn.
丁　汉生：　您可以给我打电话，也可以给我发电子 邮件。

Jiékè:　　　Hǎo de !
杰　克：　好的！

2.2

Dōngfāng Xuéyuàn Hěn Dà , Yě Hěn Piàoliang

东方 学院 很 大，也 很 漂亮

Eastern College is big and beautiful

Preliminary exercises

1. **Warm up**

Have you ever been the guest of a Chinese family? How do Chinese people usually entertain a guest?

Do you think the Chinese language is difficult or not?

How do you feel about your Chinese school?

2. **Learn the following words and form correct sentences with the words under the teacher's guidance.**

（1）请 坐

（2）怎么样 公司 你的

（3）朋友 女 我的 是 这

（4）他 漂亮 很 的 女朋友

（5）你 喝 中国茶 喜欢 吗

（6）我 学习 中文系 东方学院 英国 在

3. **Learn the following words and choose the correct answer to fill in the blanks according to the recording.**

请 大 好 漂亮

（1）_____ 进！_____ 坐！_____ 喝茶！

（2）东方学院很 _____。

（3）白小红很 _____。

（4）她男朋友很 _____。

Questions:

Should 请 be put before or after a verb?

Should 是 be used before the adjectives 好，大，漂亮 or not?

Words and expressions

1.	这	(Pron.)	zhè	this
2.	那	(Pron.)	nà	that
3.	男	(Adj.)	nán	male
4.	女	(Adj.)	nǚ	female
5.	朋友	(N.)	péngyou	friend
6.	请	(V.)	qǐng	please
7.	进	(DV.)	jìn	enter
8.	坐	(V.)	zuò	sit
9.	喝	(V.)	hē	drink
10.	茶	(N.)	chá	tea
11.	哪儿（哪里）	(QW)	nǎr (nǎlǐ)	where
12.	学院	(N.)	xuéyuàn	college
13.	系	（ N. ）	xì	department (of a university)
14.	学习	(V.)	xuéxí	study, learn
15.	怎么样	(QW)	zěnmeyàng	how
16.	大	(Adj.)	dà	big
17.	小	(Adj.)	xiǎo	small, little
18.	漂亮	(Adj.)	piàoliang	beautiful
19.	喜欢	(V.)	xǐhuan	like

Proper noun

东方学院	Dōngfāng Xuéyuàn	Eastern College

◈ Listen to the dialogue and answer the following questions. (Try best to answer in Chinese.)

（1）Whose girlfriend is Zhang Yuanyuan?

（2）Whose home is Zhang Yuanyuan staying at?

（3）Which college is Zhang Yuanyuan studying in?

（4）How does Zhang Yuanyuan feel about Eastern College?

◈ Listen to the recording while reading the text on the right. ⇨

◈ Read aloud the text and try not to look at the pinyin.

◈ Work in groups and act out the conversation.

◈ Activity:

（1）Role play: Three students play parts A, B and C. A goes to a Chinese family's house, C's, as a guest with his/her friend B. A introduces B to C and C gives them a warm welcome.

（2）Work in pairs: Where are you studying/working? How do you feel about it?

（3）Write down what you have said in Activity 2 and exchange it with your classmates through emails.

Vocabulary extension

小学	xiǎoxué	elementary school	中学	zhōngxué	middle school
大学	dàxué	university	西方	Xīfāng	the West
饮料	yǐnliào	beverage	咖啡	kāfēi	coffee
水	shuǐ	water	橙汁	chéngzhī	orange juice
可乐	kělè	Coke			

Text

Jiang Shan, and his girlfriend Zhang Yuanyuan are invited to Ding Hansheng's home.

Jiāng Shān:
江　山： 这是我的女朋友，张　园园。 *This is my girlfriend Zhang Yuanyuan.*
Zhè shì wǒ de nǚ péngyou, Zhāng Yuányuan.

Dīng Hànshēng:
丁　汉生： 你好！请进！ *Hello, Qing Jin Please Enter*
Nǐ hǎo! Qǐng jìn!

Zhāng Yuányuan:
张　园园： 好，好。 *Okay okay*
Hǎo, hǎo.

Dīng Hànshēng:
丁　汉生： 请坐。 *Please sit*
Qǐng zuò.

Jiāng Shān:
江　山： 谢谢。 *Thank you*
Xièxie.

Dīng Hànshēng:
丁　汉生： 请喝茶。 *Please drink tea*
Qǐng hē chá.

Zhāng Yuányuan:
张　园园： 好，谢谢！ *good, Thank you.*
Hǎo, xièxie!

Dīng Hànshēng:
丁　汉生： 你在哪儿学习？ *where do you study.*
Nǐ zài nǎr xuéxí?

Zhāng Yuányuan:
张　园园： 我在英国　东方　学院中文系学习。 *I study at Chinese Department at Eastern College in England*
Wǒ zài Yīngguó Dōngfāng Xuéyuàn Zhōngwénxì xuéxí.

Dīng Hànshēng:
丁　汉生： 哦。东方　学院怎么样？ *How is Eastern College.*
Ò. Dōngfāng Xuéyuàn zěnmeyàng?

Zhāng Yuányuan:
张　园园： 很好。很大，也很漂亮。我很喜欢。
Hěn hǎo. Hěn dà, yě hěn piàoliang. Wǒ hěn xǐhuan.

very good, very big, very beautiful, I like it very much.

> It is common in Chinese to omit the subject or object of a sentence, especially in spoken style.

2.3 Language Points

❧ Word stress

In Chinese most words are disyllabic, but there are some words that are monosyllabic or polysyllabic. The last syllable in monosyllabic and polysyllabic words is usually stressed except when it is in the neutral tone. The basic pattern of word stress for the majority disyllabic words is either (1) stressed-unstressed or (2) stressed final syllable.

(1) stressed-unstressed pattern

e.g.

名字 Míngzi   朋友 péngyou   喜欢 xǐhuan   漂亮 piàoliang

(2) stressed final syllable

e.g.

工作 gōngzuò   电话 diànhuà   汉语 Hànyǔ   老师 lǎoshī

❧ Place expressions

Place words are usually introduced by "zài". The zài phrases can stand as the predicate by itself, or followed by a verb, e.g.

你在哪儿?   我在英国。
Nǐ zài nǎr?   Wǒ zài Yīngguó.

你在哪儿学习?   我在英国学习。
Nǐ zài nǎr xuéxí?   Wǒ zài Yīngguó xuéxí.

In Chinese expressions of place, bigger places come before smaller ones, just the opposite of English.

the biggest ————————————————→ the smallest

中国   上海   复旦   大学
Zhōngguó   Shànghǎi   Fùdàn   Dàxué
Fudan University, Shanghai, China

❧ Simple sentence pattern 2: Subject + Adjective

In Chinese adjectives are similar to verbs in function, so they can be used directly as predicates without the copulative verb "to be".

Subject + Adjective

（1）我很高兴。
Wǒ hěn gāoxìng. *I very happy/glad*

（2）我们的大学很大，也很漂亮。
Wǒmen de dàxué hěn dà, yě hěn piàoliang. *Aur college is big and prity*

（3）我的工作不好。
Wǒ de gōngzuò bù hǎo. *My job is not good*

Note: Here "是 shì" cannot precede a predicate adjective, e.g.

A: 你的大学怎么样？　　Nǐ de dàxué zěnmeyàng? *How is your college*
B: 我的大学很大。　　　Wǒ de dàxué hěn dà. *My college is big*

很 and other adverbs always precede the predicate adjective in a statement. Here 很 does not necessarily indicate degree. If the adjective predicate is a single word, it indicates comparison, e.g.

（1）我们的大学大，他们的大学小。
Wǒmen de dàxué dà, tāmen de dàxué xiǎo. *Our college big their college is small*

（2）我的工作好，他的工作不好。
Wǒ de gōngzuò hǎo, tā de gōngzuò bù hǎo. *My work is good their work is not good*

✤ Review exercises: Choose the correct sentences.

（1）A. 我学习在东方学院。
　　　B. 我学习在东方学院。
　　　C. 我在东方学院学习。

（2）A. 我可以打电话你吗？
　　　B. 我可以给你打电话吗？
　　　C. 我可以给你打电话呢？

can I call u?

（3）A. 我在进出口公司工作。
　　　B. 我工作在进出口公司。
　　　C. 我工作在公司进出口。

（4）A. 东方学院是很大。
　　　B. 东方学院很大。
　　　C. 东方学院大。

（5）A. 请喝茶。
　　　B. 茶喝，请。
　　　C. 喝茶，请。

（6）A. 他的女朋友是不漂亮。
　　　B. 他的女朋友不是漂亮。
　　　C. 他的女朋友不漂亮。

❀ Visitors to Chinese homes are usually served hot tea under normal circumstances. Naturally, other beverages such as coffee, soda water, fruit juice, or mineral water may be served depending on the visitors' preferences, and depending on the season of the year. Alcoholic drinks, such as beer or wine, are usually served only with meals. Tap water (zìláishuǐ) when boiled (kāishuǐ) can be a preferred drink of some Chinese people.

Unit 3

Nǐ Jiā Yǒu Jǐ Kǒu Rén?
你 家 有 几 口 人?
How Many People Are There in Your Family?

Learning objectives

❋ Chatting about family and school
❋ Identifying numbers
❋ Intentions and reasons

Key sentences

Nǐ jiā yǒu jǐ kǒu rén?
你家有几口人?

How many people are there in your family?

Nǐmen xuéxiào yǒu duōshao xuésheng?
你们 学校 有 多少 学生 ?

How many students are there in your university/school?

Wǒ xiǎng, dàgài yǒu sānwàn gè.
我 想 ,大概 有 三万 个。

There are about 30 thousand, I think.

Nǐ wèi shénme xiǎng xuéxí Hànyǔ?
你 为 什么 想 学习 汉语?

Why do you want to study Chinese?

Lǎobǎn ràng wǒ qù nàr gōngzuò.
老板 让 我 去 那儿 工作。

The boss wants me to go there to work.

3.1

Háizi Hěn Kě'ài

孩子很可爱

The child is cute

Preliminary exercises

1. Warm up

What kind of family information are common topics of Chinese people?

Do you think there is any difference between modern Chinese families and traditional Chinese families?

2. Learn the following words and form correct sentences with the words under the teacher's guidance.

（1）可爱 很 孩子 这

（2）太太 我 是 这 的

（3）几 人 有 你 家 口

（4）地方 什么 人 你 是

（5）爸爸 妈妈 你 和 在 这儿 吗 也

（6）我 有 男孩儿 女孩儿 一 个 一 个

3. Learn the following words and choose the correct answer to fill in the blanks according to the recording.

吧 啊 有 个 两 多

（1）你 _____ 大？——我 22 岁。

（2）我有 _____ 个孩子，一 _____ 男孩儿，一 _____ 女孩儿。

（3）我家只 _____ 三口人，他家 _____ 七口人。

（4）你是中国人 _____ ？——是 _____ ，我是中国人。

Questions:

What does measure word mean in Chinese? Give some examples.

What is the different function between 二 and 两?

Translate the sentence 我家有五口人 into English and compare the sentence pattern of English and Chinese.

Words and expressions

1.	地方	(N.)	dìfang	place
2.	这儿（这里）	(Pron.)	zhèr (zhèlǐ)	here
3.	有	(V.)	yǒu	have; there be
4.	几	(QW)	jǐ	how many
5.	个	(MW)	gè	a most commonly used measure word
6.	口	(MW)	kǒu	a measure word for people (when talking about family members)
7.	家	(N. & MW)	jiā	family, home
8.	爸爸	(N.)	bàba	father
9.	妈妈	(N.)	māma	mother
10.	先生	(N.)	xiānsheng	husband; Mr., sir
11.	太太	(N.)	tàitai	wife; Mrs., madame
12.	孩子	(N.)	háizi	child
	男孩儿		nánháir	boy
	女孩儿		nǚháir	girl
13.	和	(Conj.)	hé	and
14.	多大		duō dà	how old
15.	两	(Num.)	liǎng	two
16.	岁	(MW)	suì	… year(s) old
17.	可爱	(Adj.)	kě'ài	lovely, cute
18.	吧	(Part.)	ba	
19.	啊	(Part.)	a	

Proper noun

	广东	Guǎngdōng	a province of China

☼ Listen to the dialogue and answer the following questions. (Try best to answer in Chinese.)

（1）Which Chinese places are Bai Xiaohong and Ding Hansheng from?

（2）How many people are there in Ding Hansheng's family? Who are they?

（3）Is Ding Hansheng living together with his family?

（4）Does Ding Hansheng have a son or daughter? How old is his child?

☼ Listen to the recording while reading the text on the right. ⇨

☼ Read aloud the text and try not to look at the pinyin.

☼ Work in groups and act out the conversation.

☼ Activity:

(1) Bring a photo of your family to the class and introduce your family members to your classmates, including: how many members there are, who they are, where they work. Write down what you have said in Chinese and exchange it with your classmates via email.

(2) The following is a photo of Bai Xiaohong's family. Look at it and say how many members there are, guess who they are, and how old they probably are.

Vocabulary extension

爷爷	yéye	paternal grandfather	奶奶	nǎinai	paternal grandmother
外公	wàigōng	maternal grandfather	外婆	wàipó	maternal grandmother
哥哥	gēge	elder brother	姐姐	jiějie	elder sister
弟弟	dìdi	younger brother	妹妹	mèimei	younger sister
年纪	niánjì	age			

Text

Bai Xiaohong and Ding Hansheng have just met each other. By chance, both of them come from Guangdong Province, China. This makes them feel close.

Bái Xiǎohóng : Nǐ shì shénme dìfang rén ?
白小红： 你是什么地方人？ *where are you from?*

Dīng Hànshēng : Wǒ shì Guǎngdōngrén, nǐ ne ?
丁 汉生： 我是 广东人，你呢？ *I am Cantonese/How about you?*

Bái Xiǎohóng : Wǒ yě shì Guǎngdōngrén.
白小红： 我也是 广东人。 *I'm also Cantonese.*

Dīng Hànshēng : Nǐ yí gè rén zài zhèr ?
丁 汉生： 你一个人在这儿？ *are you the only one here?*

Bái Xiǎohóng : Yí gè rén. Nǐ ne ?
白小红： 一个人。你呢？ *I am the only one here. How about you.*

Dīng Hànshēng : Wǒ yì jiā rén dōu zài zhèr .
丁 汉生： 我一家人都在这儿。 *All family is here*

> Here "一家人 yì jiā rén" means the whole family.

Bái Xiǎohóng : Nǐ jiā yǒu jǐ kǒu rén ?
白小红： 你家有几口人？ *How many people are in your family*

> When talking about family members "几个人 jǐ gè rén" can be replaced by "几口人 jǐ kǒu rén".

Dīng Hànshēng : Wǔ kǒu . Wǒ bàba , māma , wǒ hé wǒ tàitai , yí gè háizi .
丁 汉生： 五口。我爸爸、妈妈，我和我太太，一个孩子。 *We have 5 people, my dad, me and mom, my wife, an me child*

Bái Xiǎohóng : Nánháir háishi nǚháir ?
白小红： 男孩儿还是女孩儿？ *Boy or girl?*

Dīng Hànshēng : Nǚháir .
丁 汉生： 女孩儿。 *Girl.*

Bái Xiǎohóng : Háizi duō dà ?
白小红： 孩子多大？ *How old is the child?*

> This is the same as "孩子两岁 háizi liǎng suì". When one talks about age, no verb is needed in the sentence. "Two" is usually read "两 liǎng" before measure words.

Dīng Hànshēng : Liǎng suì .
丁 汉生： 两岁。 *2 years old*

> "吧 ba" here implies supposition.

Bái Xiǎohóng : Hěn kě'ài ba ?
白小红： 很可爱吧？ *is she very cute?*

Dīng Hànshēng : shì a , hěn kě'ài.
丁 汉生： 是啊，很可爱。 *Yes, she very cute.*

> Here "啊 a" is used to relax the tone.

3.2

Nǐmen Xuéxiào Yǒu Duōshao Xuésheng?

你们 学校 有 多少 学生？

How many students are there in your university?

↓ **Preliminary exercises**

1️⃣ **Warm up**

Approximately how many students are there in your school? How many are studying Chinese?

Why do you want to study Chinese?

2️⃣ Learn the following words and form correct sentences with the words under the teacher's guidance.

（1）多少 学生 你们 学校 有

（2）两 百 人 个 我们 公司 有 大概

（3）学习 汉语 有 没有 人 你们 公司

（4）你 去 中国 想 为什么

（5）老板 让 我 工作 中国 去 因为

（6）公司 让 我 学习 汉语 来 这儿

3️⃣ Complete the sentences according to the recording.

（1）我想去你们公司 _____。　　（2）老板让我 _____。

（3）那儿没有人 _____。　　　　（4）我们学校有很多人 _____。

4️⃣ Write down the numbers according to the recording.

_____　_____　_____　_____

Questions:

Is the successive use of verbs allowed in Chinese?

What is the negative form of 有?

What is the difference between reading Chinese numbers and English numbers?

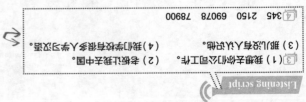

Listening script

③（1）我想去你们公司工作。　　（2）老板让我去中国。

（3）那儿没有人认识他。　　　　（4）我们学校有很多人学习汉语。

④345　2150　69078　78900

Words and expressions

1.	学校	(N.)	xuéxiào	school; educational institution
2.	学生	(N.)	xuésheng	student
3.	多少	(QW)	duōshao	how many; how much
4.	大概	(Adv.)	dàgài	maybe; about
5.	百	(Num.)	bǎi	hundred
6.	千	(Num.)	qiān	thousand
7.	万	(Num.)	wàn	ten thousand
8.	没有	(V.)	méiyǒu	not have
9.	多	(Adj.)	duō	many, much
10.	少	(Adj.)	shǎo	few, little
11.	想	(V. & MV)	xiǎng	think; want to (do sth.)
12.	让	(V.)	ràng	let
13.	去	(V.)	qù	go
14.	来	(V.)	lái	come
15.	那儿（那里）	(Pron.)	nàr (nàlǐ)	there
16.	为什么		wèi shénme	why
	为	(Prep.)	wèi	for
17.	因为		yīnwèi	because
18.	分公司		fēngōngsī	branch of a company
19.	老板	(N.)	lǎobǎn	boss

⚙ Listen to the dialogue and answer the following questions. (Try best to answer in Chinese.)

（1）How many students are there in Zhang Lin's college?

（2）Are there many students who are learning Chinese in Zhang Lin's college? About how many?

（3）Why does Jack want to learn Chinese? Where does he want to learn it?

⚙ Listen to the recording while reading the text on the right. ⇨

⚙ Read aloud the text and try not to look at the pinyin.

⚙ Work in groups and act out the conversation.

⚙ Activity:

（1）Speaking practice: How many students are there in your class? How many in your school or company? How many are studying Chinese?

（2）Speaking practice: Why do you want to study Chinese?

Vocabulary extension

亿	yì	a hundred million	重要	zhòngyào	important
有用	yǒuyòng	useful	有意思	yǒu yìsi	interesting
经济	jīngjì	economy	文化	wénhuà	culture
对…	duì …	be interested in …			
有兴趣	yǒu xìngqù				

_____   _____

_____   _____

Text

Jack's company intends to send Jack to China, so he starts to learn Chinese at a university in his spare time.

Jiékè： Nǐmen xuéxiào yǒu duōshao xuésheng?
杰 克： 你们学校有多少 学生？ — *How many students are here in you school*

Zhāng Lín： Wǒ xiǎng, dàgài yǒu sānwàn gè.
张 林： 我 想，大概有 三万个。

> Here 想 is used as an ordinary verb and means "think".

I think, about 30,000 students.

Jiékè： Yǒu méiyǒu rén xuéxí Hànyǔ?
杰 克： 有 没有人学习汉语？ — *Does anyone learn Mandrin?*

Zhāng Lín： Yǒu hěn duō rén xuéxí Hànyǔ.
张 林： 有 很 多人学习汉语。

> 多 by itself cannot precede nouns. It must be used together with 很.

There are many people learning Mandirin

Jiékè： Dàgài yǒu duōshao rén?
杰 克： 大概有 多少人？ — *How many students?* *around*

Jiāng Shān： Dàgài yǒu yìqiān gè.
张 林： 大概有一千个。 — *About 1000.*

Jiékè： Wǒ xiǎng qù nǐmen xuéxiào xuéxí Hànyǔ.
杰 克： 我 想 去你们学校学习汉语。 —

> Here 想 means "wish to" and functions as a modal verb followed by another verb or verb phrase.

— I want to go your school learn Mandirin

Jiāng Shān： Shì ma? Nǐ wèi shénme xiǎng xuéxí Hànyǔ?
张 林： 是吗？你为什么 想学习汉语？ — *Really? why do you want to learn Mandirin*

Jiékè： Wǒmen zài zhōngguó yǒu yí gè fēn gōngsī, lǎobǎn ràng wǒ qù nàr
杰 克： 我们在 中国 有一个分公司，老板让我去那儿

gōngzuò.
工作。 — *Our branch is in china boss let me go there to work.*

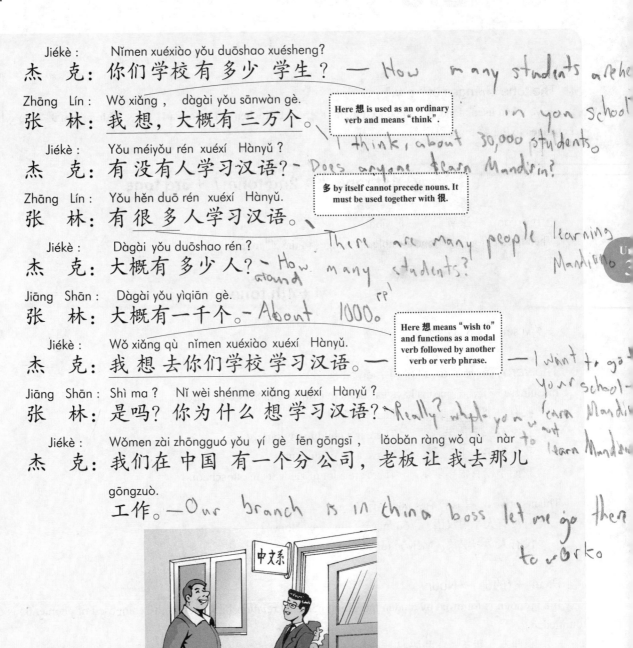

3.3 Language Points

❧ **The tone changes of "一 yī"**

一 yī, when used alone, is pronounced in the 1st tone. But when put before a 1st tone, 2nd tone or a 3rd tone syllable, it changes to the 4th tone.

> **yì + 1st tone / + 2nd tone / + 3rd tone**

一千 yìqiān   一家 yì jiā   一百 yìbǎi
When used before a 4th tone syllable, it changes to the 2nd tone.

> **yí + 4th tone**

一岁 yí suì   一个 yí gè

❧ **The verb "有 yǒu" and "没有 méiyǒu"**

In Chinese "有 yǒu" means have/has or there is/there are. So we can say:

我有一个孩子。   I have a child.
我家有一个孩子。   There is a child in my family.
我有很多学生。   I have a lot of students.
我们学校有很多学生。 There are a lot of students in our school.

The negative of 有 is 没有，not 不有，e.g.
有没有人学习汉语？Yǒu méiyǒu rén xuéxí Hànyǔ?
没有人学习汉语。Méiyǒu rén xuéxí Hànyǔ.

❧ **Pron. + (的de) + Noun**

If a pronoun is followed by a noun indicating personal relationships or an entity composed of people, 的 is often omitted, e.g.

我朋友 我爸爸 我妈妈 我太太
我家 我国 我们学校 我们公司

❧ **Numbers**

0	1	2	3	4	5	6	7	8	9	10
（○）	一	二	三	四	五	六	七	八	九	十
líng	yī	èr	sān	sì	wǔ	liù	qī	bā	jiǔ	shí

11 十一 shíyī	12 十二 shí'èr	13····························· 十三 shísān		20 二十 èrshí
21 二十一 èrshíyī	22 二十二 èrshí'èr	23····························· 二十三 èrshísān		30 三十 sānshí
	·····························			40 四十 sìshí
	·····························			100 一百 yìbǎi
101 一百零一 yìbǎi líng yī	102 一百零二 yìbǎi líng èr	·····························		110 一百一十 yìbǎi yīshí
111 一百一十一 yìbǎi yīshíyī	112 一百一十二 yìbǎi yīshí'èr	·····························		120 一百二十 yìbǎi èrshí
				200 二百 èrbǎi
				300 三百 sānbǎi
				1000 一千 yìqiān
				10,000 一万 yíwàn

Note: 10,000 should be read " 一万 yíwàn"instead of " 十千 shíqiān". 100,000 is " 十万 shíwàn" and 1,000,000 is " 一百万 yìbǎiwàn".

The number two is usually read " 两 liǎng"before measure words, instead of " 二 èr", e.g.

两个人 liǎng gè rén   two persons

❀ Measure Words（Ⅰ）

A measure word should be inserted between a number and a noun. Different nouns are combined with different measure words. "个 gè" is the most widely used measure word.

Num. + MW + N.

一个人 yí gè rén   三百个学生 sānbǎi gè xuésheng
两个地方 liǎng gè dìfang   五个公司 wǔ gè gōngsī
六个大学 liù gè dàxué   五口人 wǔ kǒu rén

❀ "几 jǐ" and "多少 duōshao"

Both "几 jǐ" and "多少 duōshao" are used to ask "how many". 几 is used to ask about a small number; a measure word should be inserted between 几 and the noun; e.g. "几个人 jǐ gè rén". 多少 can be used to ask about any number; a measure word may be used but often omitted between 多少 and the noun; e.g. "多少人 duōshao rén".

❀ Verb phrases in series

In Chinese two or more verbal phrases can be used in a series within one sentence.

… VP₁ + VP₂ …

There are two types of sentences of this sort. The first consists of two or more verbal phrases sharing the same subject, e.g.

我　想　去你们学校　学习汉语。
Wǒ xiǎng qù nǐmen xuéxiào xuéxí Hànyǔ.

In the second sort the object of the first verbal phrase is the subject of the following verbal phrase, e.g.

在　我们　学校，有　很多人　学习汉语。
Zài wǒmen xuéxiào, yǒu hěn duō rén xuéxí Hànyǔ.

老板　让　我　去中国工作。
Lǎobǎn ràng wǒ qù Zhōngguó gōngzuò.

❀ Review exercises: Choose the correct sentences.

（1）A. 你家有几人？
　　　B. 你的家有几人？
　　　C. 你家有几口人？

（2）A. 你们学校有没有汉语老师？
　　　B. 你们学校有不有汉语老师？
　　　C. 有没有汉语老师在你们学校？

（3）A. 这女孩儿是可爱。
　　　B. 这女孩儿是很可爱。
　　　C. 这女孩儿很可爱。

（4）A. 我想学习汉语去你们学校。
　　　B. 我想学习汉语在你们学校。
　　　C. 我想去你们学校学习汉语。

（5） A. 我有二中国朋友。
B. 我有二个中国朋友。
C. 我有两个中国朋友。

（6） A. 他们公司很大，有十千个人。
B. 他们公司很大，有一万个人。
C. 他们公司是很大，有一万个人。

文化点　Wénhuà Diǎn　**Cultural notes**

The following diagram shows the terms used for members of a Chinese family.

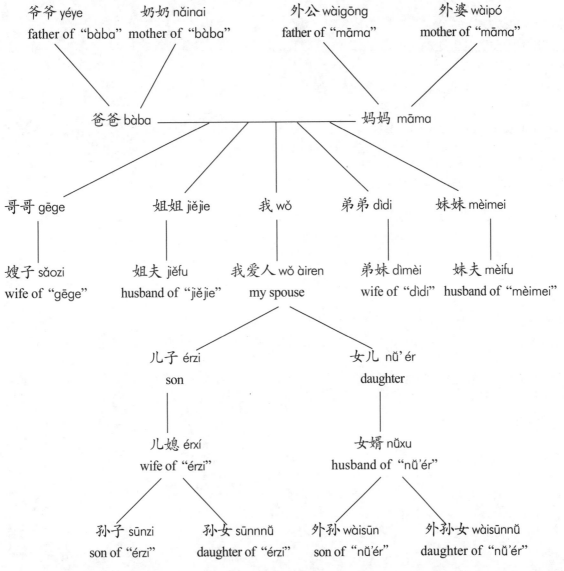

爷爷 yéye
father of "bàba"

奶奶 nǎinai
mother of "bàba"

外公 wàigōng
father of "māma"

外婆 wàipó
mother of "māma"

爸爸 bàba

妈妈 māma

哥哥 gēge

姐姐 jiějie

我 wǒ

弟弟 dìdi

妹妹 mèimei

嫂子 sǎozi
wife of "gēge"

姐夫 jiěfu
husband of "jiějie"

我爱人 wǒ àiren
my spouse

弟妹 dìmèi
wife of "dìdi"

妹夫 mèifu
husband of "mèimei"

儿子 érzi
son

女儿 nǚ'ér
daughter

儿媳 érxí
wife of "érzi"

女婿 nǚxu
husband of "nǚ'ér"

孙子 sūnzi
son of "érzi"

孙女 sūnnnǚ
daughter of "érzi"

外孙 wàisūn
son of "nǚ'ér"

外孙女 wàisūnnǚ
daughter of "nǚ'ér"

In China, a married woman keeps her maiden name. Usually the child or children will take the father's surname, but in some cases they may use the mother's. Thus if the father's surname is Mǎ, and the mother's surname is Wáng, a child's surname may be either Mǎ or (much less commonly) Wáng.

✤ When talking about his own wife in the presence of others, the husband may call her "wǒ tàitai", "wǒ àiren" or "wǒ lǎopo". When a wife is talking to others about her husband, she may call him "wǒ xiānsheng", "wǒ àiren" or "wǒ lǎogōng". When husband and wife address each other, they may call each other by their given names.

✤ In order to control population growth, people in China's mainland follow the national one-child policy. Generally, each family has only one child.

Unit 4

Wǒ Xiǎng Qù Zhōngguó
我 想 去 中国
I Want to Go to China

Learning objectives

* Making requests
* Making comments
* Identifying possessions
* Talking about school things

Key sentences

Zhè zhāng dìtú shì Yīngwén de.
这 张 地图 是 英文 的。

This map is in English.

Zhè běn cídiǎn fēicháng hǎo , fēicháng yǒuyòng.
这 本 词典 非常 好 , 非常 有用。

This dictionary is very good and very useful.

Zhè běn cídiǎn shì nín de ma?
这 本 词典 是 您 的 吗?

Is this dictionary yours?

Wǒ kàn yíxià , xíng ma?
我 看 一下, 行 吗?

Can I have a look?

Wǒ néng bu néng yòng yíxià ?
我 能 不 能 用 一下?

May I use it for a moment?

4.1

Nǐ Yào Zhōngwén De Háishi Yīngwén De?

你要 中文 的 还是 英文 的?

Do you want the Chinese one or the English one?

Preliminary exercises

1 **Warm up**

Do you have a map of China?

Which Chinese cities do you know?

Do you want to have a visit to China?

2 **Learn the following words and form correct sentences with the words under the teacher's guidance.**

（1）龙山 他 家 在 我 知道

（2）地方 比较 小 那 个

（3）我 中国 玩儿 去 想

（4）有意思 真 名字 个 这

（5）地图 英文 的 中国 请 给 一 张 我

3 **Learn the following words and choose the correct answer to fill in the blanks according to the recording.**

干什么 一下 的

（1）你想去中国 _____ ？

（2）我可以看 _____ 吗？

（3）请让我想 _____ 。

（4）我有两张中国地图，一张是英文 _____ ，一张是中文 _____ 。

Questions:

What does 干什么 mean?

What do 英文的 and 中文的 mean? Do they have English equivalents?

What does 一下 mean? What kind of tone is presented in the "V 一下" sentence construction?

3 （1）你想去中国干什么？
（2）我可以看一下吗？
（3）请让我想一下。
（4）我有两张中国地图，一张是英文的，一张是中文的。

Listening script

Words and expressions

1.	地图	(N.)	dìtú	map
2.	张	(MW)	zhāng	a measure word for paper/map/ticket
3.	中文	(N.)	Zhōngwén	Chinese language
4.	英文	(N.)	Yīngwén	English language
5.	要	(V. & MV)	yào	want (sth./to do sth.); be going to do sth.
6.	干	(V.)	gàn	do
7.	看	(V.)	kàn	look
8.	给	(V.)	gěi	give
9.	玩儿	(V.)	wánr	play; do sth. for pleasure
10.	知道	(V.)	zhīdào	know
11.	一下		yíxià	used after a verb indicating one action or one try
12.	行	(V.)	xíng	OK; all right
13.	有意思		yǒu yìsi	interesting
	意思	(N.)	yìsi	meaning
14.	比较	(Adv.)	bǐjiào	comparatively, fairly
15.	真	(Adv.)	zhēn	really
16.	龙	(N.)	lóng	dragon
17.	山	(N.)	shān	mountain, hill

Proper nouns

1.	北京	Běijīng	Beijing
2.	上海	Shànghǎi	Shanghai
3.	龙山	Lóngshān	Longshan

Unit
4

⚙ Listen to the dialogue and answer the following questions. (Try best to answer in Chinese.)

（1）Why does Jiang Shan want to look at a map of China?

（2）Does he want to look at a Chinese map or an English one?

（3）Where is Bai Xiaohong's hometown?

⚙ Listen to the recording while reading the text on the right. ⇨

⚙ Read aloud the text and try not to look at the pinyin.

⚙ Work in groups and act out the conversation.

⚙ Activity:

（1）Work in pairs. Look at a map of China. One student says place names and the other finds them on the map.

（2）Discussion: If you have a chance to visit China, where do you wish to go?

Vocabulary extension

省	shěng	province	自治区	zìzhìqū	autonomous region
市	shì	city	县	xiàn	county
镇	zhèn	town	旅游	lǚyóu	to tour
北方	běifāng	northen area	南方	nánfāng	southern area
护照	hùzhào	passport	签证	qiānzhèng	visa
_____		_____	_____		_____
_____		_____	_____		_____

Text

Jiang Shan wants to borrow a map of China from Bai Xiaohong.

Jiāng Shān : Nǐ yǒu méiyǒu Zhōngguó dìtú ?
江　山 : 你有没有 中国地图？

Bái Xiǎohóng : Yǒu . Wǒ yǒu liǎng zhāng Zhōngguó dìtú .
白小红 : 有。我有 两 张 中国 地图。

Yì zhāng Zhōngwén de , yì zhāng Yīngwén de .
一张 中文的, 一张 英文的。

> This means "一张中文的中国地图，一张英文的中国地图". The noun in "… 的 +N." is omitted.

Jiāng Shān : Wǒ kàn yíxià , xíng ma ?
江　山 : 我看一下，行吗？

Bái Xiǎohóng : Xíng . Nǐ yào Zhōngwén de háishi Yīngwén de ?
白小红 : 行。你要 中文 的还是英文的？

Jiāng Shān : Yīngwén de .
江　山 : 英文的。

Bái Xiǎohóng : Gěi. Zhè zhāng dìtú shì Yīngwén de .
白小红 : 给。这 张 地图是 英文 的。

Jiāng Shān : Xièxie !
江　山 : 谢谢！

> "给 gěi", to give, here means here you are.

Bái Xiǎohóng : Nǐ kàn Zhòngguó dìtú gān shénme ? Nǐ xiǎng qù Zhōngguó ?
白小红 : 你看 中国 地图干什么？你 想 去中国 ？

Jiāng Shān : Shì de , Wǒ xiǎng qù Zhōngguó wánr .
江　山 : 是的，我 想 去中国 玩儿。

Bái Xiǎohóng : Nà hǎo ā ! Nǐ kàn, zhè shì Běijīng .
白小红 : 那好啊！ (unfolding the map) 你看，这是北京。

Jiāng Shān : Wǒ zhīdào .
江　山 : 我知道。

Bái Xiǎohóng : Zhè shì Shànghǎi .
白小红 : 这是 上海。

Jiāng Shān : Wǒ zhīdào .
江　山 : 我知道。

Bái Xiǎohóng : Zhè shì Lóngshān .
白小红 : 这是龙山。

Jiāng Shān : Lóngshān ? Bù zhīdào . Lóngshān dà bu dà ?
江　山 : 龙山？不知道。龙山 大不大？

Bái Xiǎohóng:　Bǐjiào xiǎo. Wǒ jiā zài nàr.

白 小 红：比较 小。我 家 在 那儿。

Jiāng Shān:　Zhè ge míngzi zhēn yǒu yìsi!　Nàr yǒu lóng ma?

江　山：这个 名字 真 有 意思！那儿 有 龙 吗？

Bái Xiǎohóng:　Nàr méiyǒu lóng, zhǐ yǒu shān.

白 小 红：那儿 没有 龙，只 有 山。

> "真 zhēn…", truly/ really…, is used commonly in exclamations.

4.2

Zhè Běn Cídiǎn Fēicháng Yǒuyòng
这 本 词典 非常 有用
This dictionary is very useful

Preliminary exercises

1. **Warm up**

   Do you often use a dictionary?

   Do you have a Chinese/English dictionary? If so, is it a useful study tool?

2. Learn the following words and form correct sentences with the words under the teacher's guidance.

   （1）书 这 是 谁 的 请问

   （2）这 词典 是 大概 老师 的

   （3）有用 非常 词典 本 这

   （4）笔 你 我 的 能 不能 用 一下

3. Learn the following words and choose the correct answer to fill in the blanks according to the recording.

   本 支 个 这 那 哪

   （1）_____ 两 _____ 词典都很有用。

   （2）你们在_____ 教室上课？

   （3）_____ 笔是我的，_____ 笔是江山的。

   Questions:

   What are the measure words you have learned? What Chinese patterns are these measure words put in?

Words and expressions

1.	上课		shàngkè	attend class
2.	词典	(N.)	cídiǎn	dictionary
	汉英词典		Hàn-Yīng cídiǎn	Chinese-English dictionary
	英汉词典		Yīng-Hàn cídiǎn	English-Chinese dictionary
3.	书	(N.)	shū	book
4.	本	(MW)	běn	a measure word for books
5.	本子	(N.)	běnzi	notebook
6.	笔	(N.)	bǐ	tool for writing or drawing such as pen, pencil, etc.
7.	支	(MW)	zhī	a measure word for pen, pencil etc.
8.	教室	(N.)	jiàoshì	classroom
9.	请问		qǐngwèn	excuse me (used to begin a question)
	问	(V.)	wèn	ask
10.	能	(MV)	néng	can
11.	用	(V.)	yòng	use
12.	有用	(Adj.)	yǒuyòng	useful
13.	对	(Adj.)	duì	correct; yes
14.	非常	(Adv.)	fēicháng	very; very much
15.	谁	(QW)	shéi/shuí	who
16.	当然	(Adv.)	dāngrán	of course

⚙ Listen to the dialogue and answer the following questions. (Try best to answer in Chinese.)

(1) Whose is that Chinese-English dictionary? Whose is that English-Chinese dictionary?

(2) What does Mr. Zhang think of his dictionary?

(3) What does Martin ask Mr. Zhang?

⚙ Listen to the recording while reading the text on page 82. ⇨

⚙ Read aloud the text and try not to look at the pinyin.

⚙ Work in groups and act out the conversation.

⚙ Activity:

(1) Show your classmates your Chinese dictionary and explain its usefulness to them.

(2) Role play: Try to borrow a map/dictionary/computer from a classmate using the following words 是你的吗 , 能不能 , V 一下.

Vocabulary extension

课本	kèběn	textbook	黑板	hēibǎn	blackboard
电脑	diànnǎo	computer	台	tái	a measure word for computer, TV, etc.
教师	jiàoshī	teacher	录像	lùxiàng	video
录音	lùyīn	recording	听	tīng	to listen
语言实验室	yǔyán shíyànshì	language lab			

_____   _____

_____   _____

Unit 4

Text

Jiang Shan and Martin are in the classroom.

Mǎdīng:
马 丁: Zhè shì shénme cídiǎn?
这是什么词典?

Jiāng Shān:
江 山: Hàn-Yīng cídiǎn.
汉英 词典。

Mǎdīng:
马 丁: Nà běn ne?
那本呢?

Jiāng Shān:
江 山: Yīng-Hàn cídiǎn.
英汉 词典。

Mǎdīng:
马 丁: Zhè liǎng běn cídiǎn dōu shì nǐ de ma?
这 两 本词典都是你的吗?

Jiāng Shān:
江 山: Zhè běn Hàn-Yīng cídiǎn shì wǒ de, nà běn Yīng-Hàn cídiǎn bú shì
这本 汉英 词典是我的, 那本 英汉 词典不是
wǒ de.
我的。

Mǎdīng:
马 丁: Shì shuí de?
是 谁的?

Jiāng Shān:
江 山: Bù zhīdào. Wǒ xiǎng, zhè dàgài shì lǎoshī de cídiǎn.
不知道。我 想, 这大概是老师的词典。

Mǎdīng:
马 丁: Lǎoshī, qǐngwèn, zhè běn cídiǎn shì nín de ma?
老师, 请问, 这本 词典是您的吗?

Zhāng Lǎoshī:
张 老师: Duì, shì wǒ de.
对, 是我的。

Mǎdīng:
马 丁: Zhè běn cídiǎn zěnmeyàng?
这本词典怎么样?

Zhāng Lǎoshī:
张 老师: Zhè běn cídiǎn fēicháng hǎo, fēicháng yǒuyòng.
这本词典非常 好, 非常 有用。

Mǎdīng:
马 丁: Wǒ néng bu néng yòng yíxià?
我 能 不 能 用一下?

Zhāng Lǎoshī:
张 老师: Dāngrán kěyǐ.
当然 可以。

> The modal verb "能 néng" here refers to permission, meaning "可以 kěyǐ". But when it indicates permission, "能 néng" is usually used in questions and negative sentences.

4.3 Language Points

❀ Measure word (II)

As mentioned before, a measure word should be used between a numeral and a noun, e.g.

两本词典 liǎng běn cídiǎn

"这 zhè" or "那 nà" can be used before this construction to make it definite; a question is formed by using "哪 nǎ".

这 / 那 / 哪 + Num. + MW + N.

你要哪两本词典？这两本还是那两本词典？
Nǐ yào nǎ liǎng běn cídiǎn? Zhè liǎng běn háishi nà liǎng běn cídiǎn?

我不要这两本词典，我要那两本。
Wǒ bú yào zhè liǎng běn cídiǎn, wǒ yào nà liǎng běn.

When the numeral is 一, it is often omitted.
你喜欢哪本？这本还是那本？
Nǐ xǐhuan nǎ běn? Zhè běn háishi nà běn?

我喜欢这本，不喜欢那本。
Wǒ xǐhuan zhè běn, bù xǐhuan nà běn.

❀ Simple sentence patterns (a summary)

A. Subject + Verb (+ Object).

我去。Wǒ qù.
我学习汉语。Wǒ xuéxí Hànyǔ.
我是江山的朋友。Wǒ shì Jiāng Shān de péngyou.
我有一张中国地图。Wǒ yǒu yì zhāng Zhōngguó dìtú.
我想去你们学校学习汉语。 Wǒ xiǎng qù nǐmen xuéxiào xuéxí Hànyǔ.

The negative is formed by putting 不 in front of the verb.
我不去。Wǒ bú qù .
我不是江山的朋友。Wǒ bú shì Jiāng Shān de péngyou.
我不想去你们学校学习汉语。 Wǒ bù xiǎng qù nǐmen xuéxiào xuéxí Hànyǔ.

But the negative form of 有 is 没有. Note that 不有 is not acceptable in Chinese, e.g.
我没有中国地图。Wǒ méiyǒu Zhōngguó dìtú.

Adverbials should be used before the verb.

我们都在中文系学习汉语。Wǒmen dōu zài Zhōngwénxì xuéxí Hànyǔ.

B.   Subject + Adjective (adjectives as verbs), e.g.

她的工作不好。Tā de gōngzuò bù hǎo.

他们学校很大。Tāmen xuéxiào hěn dà.

那个地方非常小。Nà ge dìfang fēicháng xiǎo.

这本词典比较有用。Zhè běn cídiǎn bǐjiào yǒuyòng.

Generally speaking, verb 是 is not used before the adjective, but adverbs such as 不，很，非常，比较 etc., are often used to modify it.

❖ "V + 一下"

"V + 一下" indicates an instantaneous act, or doing something once quickly. It is often used to relax the tone in the sentence, expressing a suggestion or proposal, e.g.

请你看一下。Qǐng nǐ kàn yíxià.

请让我想一下。Qǐng ràng wǒ xiǎng yíxià.

❖ Review exercises: Choose the correct sentences.

（1）A. 那儿不有龙，只有山。
　　　B. 那儿没有龙，有只山。
　　　C. 那儿没有龙，只有山。

（2）A. 这张地图是英文。
　　　B. 这张地图是英文的。
　　　C. 这个地图是英文的。

（3）A. 这两词典都是有用。
　　　B. 都这两本词典很有用。
　　　C. 这两本词典都很有用。

（4）A. 谁的是这本书？
　　　B. 这本书是谁的？
　　　C. 谁的书是这本？

（5）A. 我也想去中国玩儿。
　　　B. 我也想去玩儿在中国。
　　　C. 也我想去中国玩儿。

（6）A. 我看一下，行吗？
　　　B. 我看一下，能吗？
　　　C. 我看一下，可以呢？

文化点　Wénhuà Diǎn　Cultural notes

❖ China covers an area of 9,600,000 square kilometers. The longest river in China is the Yangzi (Yangtze) River, Chángjiāng; the second longest is the Yellow River, Huánghé. China has a population of about 1.3 billion, or about 22% of the world's population. China is a multi-ethnic country with 56 ethnic groups. The Han group makes up about 93% of the whole population.

❖ According to ancient Chinese legend, 龙 lóng, or dragon, is a large, scaled serpentine creature with two horns and four clawed feet; they have the ability to not only walk, but fly and swim. Chinese dragons are water spirits with the power over the creation of rain and other weather phenomena. Dragons differ greatly from their Western counterparts in Chinese culture, as they are benevolent spirits and symbols of wealth, power, prosperity, and luck. Modern Chinese people call themselves the descendants of the dragon, or 龙的传人 (lóng de chuánrén). Depictions of dragons are common throughout China.

Unit 5

Néng Bu Néng Piányi Diǎnr ?
能 不 能 便宜 点儿?
Can You Make It Cheaper?

Learning objectives

* Shopping
* Dining
* Making suggestions
* Preference, permission and ability

Key sentences

Wǒ huì shuō yìdiǎnr Hànyǔ.

我 会 说 一点儿 汉语。

I can speak a little Chinese.

Zhè jiàn bái chènshān duōshao qián?

这 件 白 衬衫 多少 钱?

How much is this white shirt?

Néng bu néng piányi (yì) diǎnr?

能 不 能 便宜（一）点儿?

Can you make it a bit cheaper?

Wǒ néng bu néng shì yi shì?

我 能 不 能 试一试?

May I try?

Nǐmen fàndiàn zuì hǎochī de cài shì shénme?

你们 饭店 最 好吃 的 菜 是 什么?

What's the most delicious dish in your restaurant?

5.1

Zhè Jiàn Bái Chènshān Duōshao Qián?

这 件 白 衬衫 多少 钱？

How much is this white shirt?

Preliminary exercises

1　Warm up

Recall how to ask prices in Chinese as you learned in Unit 0.

Where can you bargain when shopping in China?

Get to know the value of the renminbi in China and guess how much the following items are sold for.

_____ 元　　　_____ 元　　　_____ 元　　　_____ 元

2　Learn the following words and form correct sentences with the words under the teacher's guidance.

（1）衣服 多少 钱 这 件
（2）便宜 一点儿 能 能 不
（3）试 试 一 可以 可以 不
（4）商店 这 个 衬衫 裤子 卖 只 和
（5）衬衫 那 件 白 比较 便宜，比较 漂亮 也

3　Learn the following words and choose the correct answer to fill in the blanks according to the recording.

太……了 和 还 也 件 条 试

（1）这儿的东西 ____ 贵 ____！　　　（2）这本词典 ____ 好 ____！
（3）这件衬衫很便宜，____ 很漂亮。　　（4）我想买一 ____ 衣服 ____ 一 ____ 裤子。
（5）我想买一件衬衫，____ 想买一条裤子。　　（6）您 _____ 这件怎么样？

Questions:

What is the difference of 和, 还 and 也？

What changes occur in the tone if a verb is reduplicated?

Listening script

【3】（1）这儿的东西太贵了！　　（2）这本词典太好了！
（3）这件衣服很便宜，也很漂亮。
（4）我想买一件衣服和一条裤子。
（5）我想买一件衬衫，还想买一条裤子。　（6）您试试这件怎么样？

Words and expressions

1.	商店	(N.)	shāngdiàn	shop
2.	营业员	(N.)	yíngyèyuán	shop assistant
	营业	(V.)	yíngyè	(service) be open
3.	东西	(N.)	dōngxi	thing
4.	衣服	(N.)	yīfu	clothes
5.	衬衫	(N.)	chènshān	shirt
6.	件	(MW)	jiàn	a measure word for coats
7.	裤子	(N.)	kùzi	trousers, pants
8.	条	(MW)	tiáo	a measure word for trousers, skirts, roads, rivers, fish, etc.
9.	会	(MV)	huì	can; have the skill (to do sth.)
10.	买	(V.)	mǎi	buy
11.	卖	(V.)	mài	sell
12.	试	(V.)	shì	try
13.	白	(Adj.)	bái	white
14.	红	(Adj.)	hóng	red
15.	贵	(Adj.)	guì	expensive
16.	便宜	(Adj.)	piányi	cheap
17.	钱	(N.)	qián	money
18.	块（元）	(MW)	kuài (yuán)	unit of renminbi
19.	太	(Adv.)	tài	excessively, too; more than enough
	太……了！		tài…le	It's so/too…!
	不太…		bú tài…	not too…
20.	还	(Adv.)	hái	as well; in addition
21.	一点儿		yìdiǎnr	a little
22.	那	(Conj.)	nà	In that case…; Well then…

Un
5

⚙ Listen to the dialogue and answer the following questions. (Try best to answer in Chinese.)

（1）What does Jack want to buy?

（2）How much is that white shirt? And how much is that red one?

（3）Is Jack satisfied with the pants?

⚙ Listen to the recording while reading the text on the right. ⇨

⚙ Read aloud the text and try not to look at the pinyin.

⚙ Work in groups and act out the conversation.

⚙ Activity

Role play: Give the prices in renminbi for the following items. Act out shopping in China as a shop assistant and a customer.

_____元   _____元   _____元/斤   _____元/斤

Vocabulary extension

裙子	qúnzi	skirt		大衣	dàyī	overcoat
苹果	píngguǒ	apple		香蕉	xiāngjiāo	banana
公斤	gōngjīn	kilogram		斤	jīn	1 *jin* = 500g
穿	chuān	to wear; put on		颜色	yánsè	color
蓝	lán	blue		绿	lǜ	green
黄	huáng	yellow, brown		黑	hēi	black
角（毛）	jiǎo (máo)	1 *mao* = 10 cents		分	fēn	cent
人民币	rénmínbì	renminbi, name of the Chinese currency				

_____   _____

_____   _____

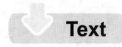

Text

Jack is in China now. Today he goes to a shop to buy clothes. The shop assistant greets him in English, but Jack responds in Chinese.

Jiékè: Nǐ hǎo!
杰 克: 你好!

Yíngyèyuán: Yō, nín huì shuō Hànyǔ?
营业员: 哟，您会说汉语?

> Here "哟 yō" is an interjection expressing a slight surprise.

Jiékè: Wǒ huì shuō yìdiǎnr.
杰 克: 我会说一点儿。

Yíngyèyuán: Xiānsheng xiǎng mǎi shénme?
营业员: 先生 想 买 什么?

Jiékè: Wǒ xiǎng mǎi yí jiàn chènshān. Zhè jiàn bái chènshān duōshao qián?
杰 克: 我 想 买一件 衬衫。这件白 衬衫 多少 钱?

Yíngyèyuán: Sìbǎi èrshíbá kuài.
营业员: 四百二十八块。

Jiékè: Tài guì le! Néng bu néng piányi diǎnr?
杰 克: 太贵了! 能 不 能 便宜点儿?

Yíngyèyuán: Bù xíng. Nà jiàn hóng chènshān bǐjiào piányi, yìbǎi liùshíwǔ kuài.
营业员: 不行。那件 红 衬衫比较 便宜，一百六十五块。

yě bǐjiào piàoliang.
也比较 漂亮。

Jiékè: Hǎo, wǒ yào nà yí jiàn.
杰 克: 好，我要那一件。

Yíngyèyuán: Nín hái yào mǎi shénme?
营业员: 您还要 买 什么?

Jiékè: Yì tiáo kùzi. Néng bu néng shì yi shì?
杰 克: 一条裤子。能 不 能 试一试?

Yíngyèyuán: Dāngrán kěyǐ.
营业员: 当然可以。

……

Yíngyèyuán: Zěnmeyàng?
营业员: 怎么样?

Jiékè: Zhè tiáo tài dà.
杰 克: 这条太大。

Yíngyèyuán: Nà nín shìshi zhè tiáo ba, zhè tiáo bú tài dà.
营业员: 那您试试这条吧，这条不太大。

Unit
5

5.2

Zuì Hǎochī De Cài Shì Shénme?

最好吃的菜是什么?

What's the most delicious dish?

Preliminary exercises

① Warm up

Can you name several Chinese dishes in Chinese? What is the difference between Chinese and Western food culture?

② Learn the following words and form correct sentences with the words under the teacher's guidance.

（1）蔬菜 喜欢 吃 他 , 肉 吃 不 爱

（2）想 你 吃 米饭 水饺 还是

（3）红烧 牛肉 好吃 最 他们 的

（4）服务 饭店 的 这 个 好 非常

（5）饭店 菜 贵 这 是 这个 最 的

③ Learn the following words and choose the correct answer to fill in the blanks according to the recording.

会　能

（1）你 _____ 说汉语吗?　（2）我 _____ 试一下吗?

（3）你 _____ 不 _____ 吃辣的?　（4）你 _____ 不 _____ 烧中国菜?

Questions:

What are the different functions of 会 and 能 ?

④ Where should 的 be placed in the following sentences?

（1）这是我太太汉语词典。　（2）你们饭店最好吃菜是什么?

（2）我朋友在中国有一个很大公司。　（3）白小红爸爸在一个大饭店工作。

Discussion:

When should 的 be used?

Words and expressions

1.	饭店	(N.)	fàndiàn	restaurant, hotel
2.	服务员	(N.)	fúwùyuán	waiter/waitress
	服务	(V. & N.)	fúwù	serve; service
3.	菜	(N.)	cài	dish
4.	糖醋鱼		tángcùyú	fish in sweet and sour sauce
	糖	(N.)	táng	sugar
	醋	(N.)	cù	vinegar
	鱼	(N.)	yú	fish
5.	酸辣汤		suānlàtāng	sour-and-spicy soup
	酸	(Adj.)	suān	sour
	辣	(Adj.)	là	spicy, hot
	汤	(N.)	tāng	soup
6.	牛肉	(N.)	niúròu	beef
	牛	(N.)	niú	cattle, ox, cow
	肉	(N.)	ròu	meat
7.	蔬菜	(N.)	shūcài	vegetable
8.	米饭	(N.)	mǐfàn	cooked rice
9.	水饺 (饺子)	(N.)	shuǐjiǎo (jiǎozi)	dumpling
10.	红烧		hóngshāo	cook in soy sauce
	烧	(V.)	shāo	cook
11.	吃	(V.)	chī	eat
12.	好吃	(Adj.)	hǎochī	delicious
13.	等	(V.)	děng	wait
14.	最	(Adv.)	zuì	the most

Unit
5

☼ Listen to the dialogue and answer the following questions. (Try best to answer in Chinese.)

（1）Where are they? What are they doing?

（2）What do they order?

（3）What is the specialty dish of the restaurant?

☼ Listen to the recording while reading the text on the right. ⇨

☼ Read aloud the text and try not to look at the pinyin.

☼ Work in groups and act out the conversation.

☼ Activity:

（1）Search online for a Chinese dish of your choice, then tell your classmates its name, and what it tastes like.

（2）Go to a Chinese restaurant and have a meal. Next, tell your classmates about the experience, what dishes did the restaurant have, and how was the food.

Vocabulary extension

鸡肉	jīròu	chicken	鸡蛋	jīdàn	egg
猪肉	zhūròu	pork	羊肉	yángròu	mutton
豆腐	dòufu	tofu	烤鸭	kǎoyā	roast duck
面	miàn	noodle	包子	bāozi	steamed stuffed bun
面包	miànbāo	bread	牛奶	niúnǎi	milk
酒	jiǔ	alcoholic drink	啤酒	píjiǔ	beer
甜	tián	sweet	咸	xián	salty
请客	qǐngkè	play the host; stand treat			
唐人街（中国城）	Tángrén Jiē（Zhōngguóchéng）	Chinatown			

_____   _____

_____   _____

Text

Bai Xiaohong, Wang Ying, Jiang Shan, Martin, etc. are traveling in China. Currenlty, they are having dinner in a restaurant.

Fúwùyuán: Qǐng zuò. ... Qǐng hē chá.
服务员：请 坐。……请喝茶。

Mǎdīng, Jiāng Shān, Bái Xiǎohóng, Wáng Yīng: Xièxie !
马丁、江山、白小红、王 英：谢谢！

Fúwùyuán: Lái yìdiǎnr shénme ?
服务员：来一点儿什么？

> 来 in this case means "cause to come", "to bring".

Mǎdīng: Nǐmen fàndiàn zuì hǎochī de cài shì shénme ?
马 丁：你们 饭店 最 好吃 的 菜 是 什么？

Fúwùyuán: Tángcùyú .
服务员：糖醋鱼。

> Here both 糖醋鱼 and 牛肉 refer to dishes, so the measure word should be 个.

Mǎdīng: Hǎo, Lái yí gè tángcùyú .
马 丁：好，来一个糖醋鱼。

Wáng Yīng: Wǒ yào chī shūcài .
王 英：我要吃蔬菜。

Fúwùyuán: Hǎo. Yào bu yào lái ge niúròu ?
服务员：好。要不要来个牛肉？

Bái Xiǎohóng: Kěyǐ. Lái yí gè hóngshāoniúròu ba .
白小红：可以。来一个红烧牛肉吧。

jiāng shān: Wǒ zuì xǐhuan chī là de , nǐmen néng bu néng chī là de ?
江 山：我 最 喜欢 吃 辣的，(to others) 你们 能 不 能 吃 辣的？

Wáng Yīng: Wǒmen dōu néng chī yìdiǎnr .
王 英：我们 都 能 吃 一点儿。

jiāng shān: Lái ge suānlàtāng .
江 山：(to the waitress) 来个酸辣汤。

> This is the same as 来一个酸辣汤，with 一 omitted.

Fúwùyuán: Hái yào shénme ?
服务员：还要 什么？

Bái Xiǎohóng: Mǐfàn .
白小红：米饭。

Mǎdīng: Shuǐjiǎo.
马 丁：水饺。

Fúwùyuán: Hǎo, qǐng děng yíxià.
服务员：好，请 等一下。

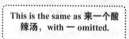

Unit 5

5.3 Language Points

❀ Lexical tones and sentence intonation

Just as every Chinese syllable has its own tone, Chinese sentences have distinct tonal patterns. As in English, the rising tone is used in yes-or-no questions in Chinese while the falling tone is used in statements. But if the last syllable of a yes-or-no question sentence is in the falling tone, or, if the last syllable of a statement is in the rising tone, what shall we do? What do we use at the end of the sentence, the rising tone or the falling tone?

Actually the sentence tone is like a large wave with many smaller waves on its surface. The overall sentence tone does not change the tones of individual words completely. Otherwise their meaning would change. Listen to the recording:

(1) 这是汤。Zhè shì tāng.

(2) 这是糖。Zhè shì táng.

❀ "能néng" and "会huì"

Both "能 néng" and "会 huì" can refer to ability. But unlike 能, 会 implies "mastering a skill by learning it", e.g.

我会用筷子（kuàizi, chopsticks）。　　Wǒ huì yòng kuàizi.

❀ "和hé", "也yě" and "还hái"

Chinese "和 hé" is not exactly the same as "and" in English. 和 is used in a very limited way. It is usually used to connect nouns or noun phrases as in "我和他 wǒ hé tā", "中国地图和美国地图 Zhōngguó dìtú hé Měiguó dìtú" but not to connect clauses, e.g.

这件衬衫很便宜，很漂亮。

Zhè jiàn chènshān hěn piányi, hěn piàoliang.

In the above sentence we can not use 和.

"也 yě" and "还 hái" not only have their own meanings but also can be used to connect clauses. 也 implies similarity between the former and the latter, e.g.

这件衬衫很便宜，也很漂亮。

Zhè jiàn chènshān hěn piányi, yě hěn piàoliang.

还 indicates supplement or addition, e.g.

我要买一件衬衫，还要买一条裤子。

Wǒ yào mǎi yí jiàn chènshān, hái yào mǎi yì tiáo kùzi.

❀ The particle "吧ba"

The particle "吧 ba" indicates supposition or suggestion. "吧 ba" in the following sentences expresses a supposition:

我想，你是美国人吧？Wǒ xiǎng , nǐ shì Měiguórén ba?

孩子很可爱吧？Háizi hěn kě'ài ba?

"吧 ba" in the following sentences indicates a suggestion or request.

让我去吧。 Ràng wǒ qù ba.

你试试吧。Ní shìshi ba.

❀ The reduplication of verbs

Some verbs indicating actions and active thinking processes can be reduplicated. The reduplicated form of monosyllabic verbs is "A（一）A" such as 看（一）看 kàn (yi) kàn, 想（一）想 xiǎng (yi) xiǎng, 试（一）试 shì (yi) shì. The reduplicated form of disyllabic verbs is ABAB, e.g. 学习学习 xuéxí xuéxí, 认识认识 rènshi rènshi.

The reduplication of verbs indicates actions of short duration. It can also express an attempted action. In sentences expressing suggestions or proposals it can soften the tone of speech, as in the pattern V. + 一下 yíxià, e.g.

我可以看（一）看你的中国地图吗？

Wǒ kěyǐ kàn (yi) kàn nǐ de Zhōngguó dìtú ma?

请等一下，让我想（一）想。

Qǐng děng yíxià, ràng wǒ xiǎng (yi) xiǎng.

我想跟你的同学们认识认识，可以吗？

Wǒ xiǎng gēn nǐ de tóngxuémen rènshi rènshi, kěyǐ ma?

❀ Attributives

Elements which modify and limit nouns are known as attibutives. In Chinese attributives always precede the nouns.

Attrib. + N.

我的	中国	地图	Wǒ de Zhōngguó dìtú
那件	红	衬衫	Nà jiàn hóng chènshān
我们饭店	最好吃的	菜	Wǒmen fàndiàn zuì hǎochī de cài

If the attributive implies a possessive relation, 的 is often used as in 老师的词典 lǎoshī de cídiǎn, 饭店的名字 fàndiàn de míngzi. Sometimes 的 may be omitted as in 我妈妈 wǒ māma, 我同学 wǒ tóngxué, 我家 wǒ jiā, 你们学校 nǐmen xuéxiào, 我们饭店 wǒmen fàndiàn.

When a monosyllabic adjective is used as an attributive, 的 is often omitted as in 好人 hǎo rén, 大饭店 dà fàndiàn, 红衬衫 hóng chènshān. Otherwise 的 is often used as in 好吃的菜 hǎochī de cài, 漂亮的地方 piàoliang de dìfang. If the adjective is modified by an adverb, 的 should also be used, as in 非常好的人 fēicháng hǎo de rén, 比较大的饭店 bǐjiào dà de fàndiàn, 很红的衬衫 hěn hóng de chènshān.

❀ Review exercises: Choose the correct sentences.

（1） A. 我能不能试一试？
　　 B. 我会不会试一试？
　　 C. 我好不好试一试？

（2） A. 他家在一个很漂亮地方。
　　 B. 他的家在一个很漂亮地方。
　　 C. 他家在一个很漂亮的地方。

（3） A. 我们饭店的酸辣汤辣和酸。
　　 B. 我们的饭店酸辣汤是辣和酸。
　　 C. 我们饭店的酸辣汤很辣，也很酸。

（4） A. 我想买衬衫，和买裤子。
　　 B. 我想买衬衫，也一条裤子。
　　 C. 我想买衬衫，还想买裤子。

文化点　Wénhuà Diǎn　**Cultural notes**

❧ There are many places for Chinese people to go shopping: stores of various sizes, specialty shops, supermarkets, and all sorts of open-air markets. For grocery shopping, Chinese generally go to farmer's markets. Shops may be state-owned or privately owned. There are many stalls in open markets and farmer's markets, and all kinds of goods are sold. It can be rather crowded and noisy in these places, and price bargaining is very common.

❧ If we suggest that a friend eat with us in a restaurant, it normally means that we will be the host and will "treat" the friend. Based on the traditional spirit of "ritualized interaction", the one who does not pay will pay the next time. Some young people have adopted the practice of "going Dutch" (AA zhì), but this is not common.

❧ Whether shopping or dining in China, there is no tax to be paid on top of the purchase price, because tax is already included. In most cases, no tipping is necessary or expected.

Unit 6

Míngtiān Dǎsuàn Gàn Shénme?
明天　打算　干　什么?
What Are You Going to Do Tomorrow?

Learning objectives

* Inviting
* Plans and preference
* Identifying when and where

Key sentences

Míngtiān xīngqīliù.

明天　星期六。

Tomorrow is Saturday.

Wǒ míngtiān wǎnshang yǒu yí gè yuēhuì.

我　明天　晚上　有一个约会。

I have an appointment tomorrow evening.

Wǒ gēn nǐ yìqǐ qù.

我　跟你一起去。

I'll go with you.

Wǒ xiǎng qǐng nǐ hē kāfēi.

我　想　请你喝咖啡。

I'd like to invite you for a cup of coffee.

Míngtiān wǎnshang wǒmen zài kāfēiguǎn jiànmiàn.

明天　晚上　我们在咖啡馆　见面。

We'll meet at the coffee shop tomorrow evening.

6.1

Wǒ Míngtiān Wǎnshang Yǒu Yí Gè Yuēhuì

我 明天 晚上 有 一 个 约会

I have an appointment tomorrow evening

Preliminary exercises

1 Warm up:

(1) What day is today? How do you say the days of the week in Chinese? How do you say "last Sunday, this Sunday, next Sunday" in Chinese?

(2) Work in pairs: One says 星期一，星期二 …, the other responds with the English equivalent. Compete to see who is quicker.

(3) Does Chinese have tenses? How is a future action expressed in Chinese?

2 Learn the following words and form correct sentences with the words under the teacher's guidance.

（1）他 去 打工 要 星期天

（2）你们 干 打算 什么 明天

（3）我 没有 约会 晚上 今天

（4）他 喜欢 看 电视 家里 在

（5）我 跟 同学 去 打球 明天上午 一起

3 Fill in the blanks according to the recording.

（1）我 _____ 休息。

（2）他 _____ 工作。

（3）_____ 我们不上课。

（4）_____ 他 _____ 看电视。

Questions:

Where are "time words" and "place words" usually placed in a Chinese sentence?

Listening script

3 （1）我明天上午休息。　　　（2）他在家用口公司工作。
（3）今天上午接们不上课。　　　（4）看明天他在家里看电视。

Words and expressions

1.	今天	(TW)	jīntiān	today
2.	明天	(TW)	míngtiān	tomorrow
3.	早上	(TW)	zǎoshang	early morning
4.	上午	(TW)	shàngwǔ	morning
5.	中午	(TW)	zhōngwǔ	noon
6.	下午	(TW)	xiàwǔ	afternoon
7.	白天	(TW)	báitiān	daytime
8.	晚上	(TW)	wǎnshang	evening
9.	星期六	(TW)	xīngqīliù	Saturday
	星期	(N.)	xīngqī	week
10.	打算	(V. & N.)	dǎsuàn	plan
11.	打工		dǎgōng	work as casual worker for somebody
12.	约会	(N.& V.)	yuēhuì	appointment; make an appointment
13.	休息	(V.)	xiūxi	rest
14.	打球		dǎ qiú	play (a ball game)
	球	(N.)	qiú	ball
15.	看电视		kàn diànshì	watch TV
	电视	(N.)	diànshì	TV
16.	家里	(PW)	jiā li	at home
	里	(LW)	lǐ	in, inside
17.	跟……一起		gēn…yìqǐ	together with…
	跟	(Prep.)	gēn	with
	一起	(Adv.)	yìqǐ	together

⚙ Listen to the dialogue and answer the following questions. (Try best to answer in Chinese.)

（1）What day is it tomorrow? Do they have classes tomorrow?

（2）What will Wang Ying do in the daytime tomorrow? What will she do in the evening?

（3）What will Jiang Shan do tomorrow?

（4）What will Bai Xiaohong do? What about Martin?

⚙ Listen to the recording while reading the text on the right. ⇨

⚙ Read aloud the text and try not to look at the pinyin.

⚙ Work in groups and act out the conversation.

⚙ Activity

（1）Pair work: Tell each other what you are planning to do this Sunday.

（2）Ask your partner if he/she likes playing ball games, if so, what kind? Note that "play football" in Chinese is not "打 dǎ"，but "踢 tī".

Vocabulary extension

篮球	lánqiú	basketball	网球	wǎngqiú	tennis
橄榄球	gǎnlǎnqiú	rugby	曲棍球	qūgùnqiú	field hockey
冰球	bīngqiú	ice hockey	排球	páiqiú	volleyball
羽毛球	yǔmáoqiú	badminton	乒乓球	pīngpāngqiú	table tennis
足球	zúqiú	soccer, football	踢足球	tī zúqiú	play football
夜里	yèli	night	昨天	zuótiān	yesterday
前天	qiántiān	the day before yesterday			
后天	hòutiān	the day after tomorrow			
上网	shàngwǎng	log onto the Internet			

Text

Bai Xiaohong and the others are talking about what they are going to do during the weekend.

Bái Xiǎohóng: Míngtiān xīngqīliù, wǒmen dōu bú shàngkè.
白小红：明天 星期六，我们 都不 上课。

Nǐmen dǎsuàn gàn shénme?
你们打算 干 什么？

> It is the same as "明天是星期六 Míngtiān shì xīngqīliù". The verb "是 shì" is often omitted when talking about the time.

Jiāng Shān: Wǒ míngtiān yào qù dǎgōng.
江 山：我 明天 要去打工。

Wáng Yīng: Wǒ míngtiān wǎnshang yǒu yí gè yuēhuì.
王 英：我 明天 晚上 有一个约会。

Bái Xiǎohóng: Báitiān ne?
白小红：白天 呢？

Wáng Yīng: Zài jiā li xiūxi. Nǐ ne?
王 英：在家里休息。你呢？

Bái Xiǎohóng: Wǒ xiǎng qù dǎ qiú, nǐmen qù bu qù?
白小红：我 想 去打球，你们去不去？

Mǎdīng: Wǒ gēn nǐ yìqǐ qù.
马 丁：我跟你一起去。

Bái Xiǎohóng: Hǎo a. Wáng Yīng, nǐ qù bu qù?
白小红：好啊。王 英，你去不去？

Wáng Yīng: Bú qù. Wǒ bù xǐhuan dǎ qiú.
王 英：不去。我不喜欢打球。

Bái Xiǎohóng: Nà nǐ xǐhuan gàn shénme?
白小红：那你喜欢 干 什么？

Wáng Yīng: Wǒ xǐhuan zài jiā li kàn diànshì.
王 英：我喜欢在家里看 电视。

Unit
6

6.2

Wǒ Xiǎng Qǐng Nǐ Hē Kāfēi

我 想 请 你 喝 咖啡

I would like to invite you for a cup of coffee

Preliminary exercises

1 Warm up:

(1) What time is it? Read the following time in Chinese.

9:05 10:10 11:15 12:30 1:45 2:55

(2) One student tells the time in Chinese, and the other writes it down as quickly as possible.

2 Learn the following words and form correct sentences with the words under the teacher's guidance.

（1）我　很　忙　现在

（2）你　空儿　有　什么　时候

（3）功课　很多　有　我　今天　晚上

（4）我　朋友　位　一　看　去　晚上　明天　要

（5）我们　见面　七　点　半　晚上　今天　咖啡馆　在

3 Read after the recording of the following sentences.

（1）我 ＿＿＿＿＿＿＿＿＿＿ 有事儿。

（2）我们 ＿＿＿＿＿＿＿＿＿＿ 上课。

（3）＿＿＿＿＿＿＿＿＿＿ ，他来我家看我。

（4）＿＿＿＿＿＿＿＿＿＿ ，我在咖啡馆等你。

Discussion:

How is the order of the time words arranged if there are several in one sentence in Chinese?

Read and discuss if the character 请 means the same in the three sentences.

（1）请进。 （2）请你说汉语。 （3）我请你喝咖啡。

Words and expressions

1.	现在	(TW)	xiànzài	now
2.	时候	(N.)	shíhou	time
	什么时候		shénme shíhou	what time; when
3.	点（钟）	(MW)	diǎn(zhōng)	o'clock
4.	分	(MW)	fēn	minute
5.	刻	(MW)	kè	quarter (of an hour)
6.	半	(Num.)	bàn	half
7.	位	(MW)	wèi	a measure word used for people to show politeness
8.	事儿	(N.)	shìr	matter, affair, thing, business
9.	空儿	(N.)	kòngr	free time; spare time
10.	忙	(Adj.)	máng	busy
11.	咖啡	(N.)	kāfēi	coffee
12.	咖啡馆	(N.)	kāfēiguǎn	cafe
13.	做	(V.)	zuò	do
14.	功课	(N.)	gōngkè	schoolwork, homework
15.	见面		jiànmiàn	meet each other
16.	见	(V.)	jiàn	see, meet
17.	对不起		duìbuqǐ	sorry
18.	没关系		méi guānxi	it doesn't matter; it's OK
19.	再见	(V.)	zàijiàn	goodbye

Uni
6

⚙ Listen to the dialogue and answer the following questions. (Try best to answer in Chinese.)

（1）Why does Martin call Bai Xiaohong?

（2）What is Bai Xiaohong doing this evening?

（3）When and where will Bai Xiaohong and Martin meet?

⚙ Listen to the recording while reading the text on the right. ⇨

⚙ Read aloud the text and try not to look at the pinyin.

⚙ Work in groups and act out the conversation.

⚙ Activity: A invites B to drink coffee/tea, to eat out, to see a film, or to play a ball game. Try to fix the time and place.

Vocabulary extension

酒	jiǔ	alcohol	酒吧	jiǔbā	bar
电影	diànyǐng	movie	电影院	diànyǐngyuàn	cinema
公园	gōngyuán	park	门口	ménkǒu	entrance, doorway
不好意思	bù hǎoyìsi	sorry	抱歉	bàoqiàn	sorry
机场	jīchǎng	airport	火车站	huǒchēzhàn	railway station
接	jiē	pick up	送	sòng	see off

_____   _____

_____   _____

Text

Martin is making a phone call to invite Bai Xiaohong for a cup of coffee. Bai Xiaohong answers the telephone.

Bái Xiǎohóng: Wèi !
白小红 ：喂！

Mǎdīng: Shì Xiǎohóng ma ?
马 丁：是小红 吗？

Bái Xiǎohóng: Shì wǒ , nín nǎ wèi ?
白小红 ：是我，您哪位？

Mǎdīng: Wǒ shì Mǎdīng.
马 丁：我是马丁。

Bái Xiǎohóng: Ā , Xiǎo Mǎ ya , nǐ hǎo ! Shénme shìr ?
白小红 ：啊，小马呀，你好！什么事儿？

Mǎdīng: Wǒ xiǎng qǐng nǐ hē kāfēi .
马 丁：我 想 请你喝咖啡。

> "请 + somebody + do something" means ask/invite somebody to do something.

Bái Xiǎohóng: Shénme shíhou ?
白小红 ：什么时候？

Mǎdīng : Jīntiān wǎnshang. Xíng ma ?
马 丁：今天 晚上。行 吗？

Bái Xiǎohóng: Bù xíng , jīntiān wǎnshang wǒ bù néng gēn nǐ yìqǐ hē kāfēi .
白小红 ：不行，今天 晚上 我不能 跟你一起喝咖啡。

jīntiān wǎnshang wǒ hěn máng, wǒ yào qù kàn yí wèi péngyou, hái yào
今天 晚上 我很 忙，我要去看一位 朋友，还要

zuò gōngkè . Duìbuqǐ !
做 功课。对不起！

Mǎdīng: Méi guānxi . Míngtiān wǎnshang zěnmeyàng ?
马 丁：没关系。明天 晚上 怎么样？

Bái Xiǎohóng: Míngtiān wǎnshang wǒ yǒu kòngr . Jǐ diǎnzhōng ?
白小红 ：明天 晚上 我有空儿。几 点钟？

Mǎdīng: Bā diǎn bàn , xíng ma ?
马 丁：八点半，行 吗？

Bái Xiǎohóng: Xíng. Zài nǎr jiànmiàn ?
白小红 ：行。在哪儿 见面？

Un
6

Mǎdīng: "Míngyuè" kāfēiguǎn .

马　丁："明月"咖啡馆。

Bái Xiǎohóng: Hǎo. Míngtiān wǎnshang jiàn! Xièxie!

白小红 ：好。明天　晚上　见！谢谢！

Mǎdīng: Zàijiàn!

马　丁：再见！

Bái Xiǎohóng: Zàijiàn!

白小红 ：再见！

6.3 Language Points

✤ Expressions of time（1）

Week 星期
星期一 xīngqīyī　Monday　　　　　　星期二 xīngqī'èr　Tuesday
星期三 xīngqīsān Wednesday　　　　星期四 xīngqīsì　Thursday
星期五 xīngqīwǔ　Friday　　　　　　星期六 xīngqīliù　Saturday
星期天 / 星期日 xīngqītiān / xīngqīrì Sunday

Time of clock:

2：00　　liǎng diǎn
　　　　　liǎng diǎnzhōng

2：05　　liǎng diǎn líng wǔ fēn

2：10　　liǎng diǎn shí fēn

2：15　　liǎng diǎn shíwǔ fēn
　　　　　liǎng diǎn yí kè

2：30　　liǎng diǎn sānshí fēn
　　　　　liǎng diǎn bàn

2：45　　liǎng diǎn sìshíwǔ fēn
　　　　　liǎng diǎn sān kè
　　　　　sān diǎn chà yí kè
　　　　　chà yí kè sān diǎn

2：55　　liǎng diǎn wǔshíwǔ fēn
　　　　　sān diǎn chà wǔ fēn
　　　　　chà wǔ fēn sān diǎn

As with place words, time expressions are arranged from the largest unit to the smallest, precisely the opposite of English.

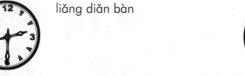

The largest　　　　　　the smallest

明天下午三点半　　　　　　　　　　　星期六上午九点三刻
míngtiān xiàwǔ sān diǎn bàn　　　　　xīngqīliù shàngwǔ jiǔ diǎn sān kè
3:30 tomorrow afternoon　　　　　　　9:45 Saturday morning

❀ Adverbials

Elements which modify or limit verbs or adjectives are known as adverbials. In Chinese adverbials should be put before verbs or adjectives.

Adverbial + V. / Adj.

Adverbs, prepositional phrases, place expressions or time expressions are commonly used as adverbials.

A. Adverb + V. / Adj.

这两本词典都是你的吗？

Zhè liǎng běn cídiǎn dōu shì nǐ de ma?

他非常忙，我不太忙。

Tā fēicháng máng, wǒ bú tài máng.

B. Prepositional phrases + V. / Adj.

我跟你一起去吧。

Wǒ gēn nǐ yìqǐ qù ba.

我可以给你打电话吗？

Wǒ kěyǐ gěi nǐ dǎ diànhuà ma?

C. Place expressions / time expressions + V. / Adj.

你在公司忙不忙？

Nǐ zài gōngsī máng bu máng?

你今天忙不忙？

Nǐ jīntiān máng bu máng?

我在家里看电视。

Wǒ zài jiā li kàn diànshì.

我们八点半上课。

Wǒmen bā diǎn bàn shàng kè.

我们明天晚上在咖啡馆见面。（明天晚上我们在咖啡馆见面。）

Wǒmen míngtiān wǎnshang zài kāfēiguǎn jiànmiàn.

（Míngtiān wǎnshang wǒmen zài kāfēiguǎn jiànmiàn.）

❀ Review exercises: Choose the correct sentences.

（1） A. 他问我去喝咖啡。
B. 他要我去喝咖啡。
C. 他请我去喝咖啡。

（2） A. 我们上课九点钟明天上午。
B. 我们九点钟明天上午上课。
C. 我们明天上午九点钟上课。

（3） A. 我们几点钟见面？
B. 我们见面几点钟？
C. 我几点钟见面你？

（4） A. 我现在在学校上课。
B. 我在学校现在上课。
C. 我上课在学校现在。

（5） A. 都老师们很忙。
B. 老师们都很忙。
C. 老师们很忙都。

（6） A. 我一起去跟你明天。
B. 我明天去一起跟你。
C. 明天我跟你一起去。

文化点　Wénhuà Diǎn　**Cultural notes**

❧ The ways Chinese address relatives are fairly complex. Members of the younger generation do not address their elders with their given names. Elders must be addressed according to their relation, for example, "younger uncle, shūshu", "elder uncle, bóbo", etc. Elders may address the younger generation directly with their names. Among people of the same generation, older individuals use given names to address those younger than them, but younger persons generally address those older than them with relation terms such as "oldest brother, dàgē", "second elder sister, èr jiě", etc.

❧ Addressing friends, schoolmates and colleagues is more casual. To address older associates, we use terms such as "old Zhang, Lǎo Zhāng", "old Li, Lǎo Lǐ", etc. To address people younger than oneself, one can use "young Zhang, Xiǎo Zhāng", "young Li, Xiǎo Lǐ", etc., or we may just use their names. Another way to address people is according to profession or social status. For example, "Mr. Zhang, Zhāng xiānsheng", "Manager Zhang, Zhāng jīnglǐ", "Instructor Zhang, Zhāng lǎoshī", "Professor Zhang, Zhāng jiàoshòu", "Mayor Zhang, Zhāng shìzhǎng", "Master Zhang, Zhāng shīfu", "Police Officer Zhang, Zhāng jǐngguān", etc.

❧ To address people we do not know, we can use "Sir, xiānsheng", "Miss, xiǎojiě", or "Master, shīfu". Sometimes, we also use terms for addressing relatives such as "older uncle, dàye" (dàbó), "older aunt, dàmā", "auntie, āyí" or "younger uncle, shūshu", etc.

❧ Now, almost all Chinese people have a cell phone. Registered users of instant communication products have reached several hundred million.

Unit 7

Nǐ Shénme Shíhou Huílái?
你 什么 时候 回来?
When Will You Come Back?

Learning objectives

- Plans and arrangements
- Identifying dates
- Worries and reassurance
- Describing people's appearance

Key sentences

Wǒ dǎsuàn qī yuè yī hào yǐqián huílái.
我 打算 七 月 一 号 以前 回来。
I will come back before July 1ˢᵗ.

Wǒ yǒu diǎnr dānxīn.
我 有 点儿 担心。
I'm a little worried.

Qǐngwèn, kěyǐ jìnlái ma?
请 问，可以 进来 吗?
Excuse me, may I come in?

Tā gāng chūqù.
她 刚 出去。
She has just gone out.

Tā shòushòu de, gāogāo de.
她 瘦瘦 的，高高 的。
She is thin and tall.

Wǒ Dǎsuàn Qī Yuè Yī Hào Yǐqián Huílái
我 打算 七月 一号 以前回来
I'll come back before July 1st

Preliminary exercises

1 Warm up

(1) What is today's date? How do you say it in Chinese? How do you say the following in Chinese: last year, this year, next year, last month, this month and next month?

(2) Activity: One student says the date in Chinese, such as 2014 年 5 月 23 号 , the other says the English equivalent. Compete to see who is quicker.

2 Learn the following words and form correct sentences with the words under the teacher's guidance.

（1）担心　你　别

（2）我　想　去　旅行　中国

（3）以前　七月一号　我们　回来

（3）以后　放假　你　打算　干　什么

（5）我　我的　朋友　你　可以　请　帮助

3 Learn the following words and choose the correct answer to fill in the blanks according to the recording.

一点儿　有点儿　还是　或者　以前　以后

（1）我可以说 _____ 汉语。　　　（2）他今天 _____ 不高兴。

（3）你这个月去 _____ 下个月去？　（4）这个月去 _____ 下个月去都可以。

（5）我晚上八点 _____ 回来。　　　（6）我晚上八点 _____ 回来。

（7）_____ 我在北京工作，现在我在上海工作，_____ 我想去四川工作。

Discussion:

1. What is the difference between 有点儿，一点儿，还是 and 或者？

2. Is there any difference between 以前，以后 and their English equivalents "before, after"?

Words and expressions

1.	今年	(TW)	jīnnián	this year
2.	放假		fàngjià	take a vacation
3.	月	(TW)	yuè	month
4.	号（日）	(WM)	hào(rì)	date
5.	上旬	(TW)	shàngxún	(during) the first ten days of a month
	中旬	(TW)	zhōngxún	(during) the middle ten days of a month
6.	下旬	(TW)	xiàxún	(during) the last ten days of a month
7.	以前	(LW)	yǐqián	before, ago
8.	以后	(LW)	yǐhòu	after, later
9.	旅行	(V.)	lǚxíng	travel
10.	回来	(DV)	huílái	come back
	回	(DV)	huí	come / go back (to a place)
11.	担心	(V.)	dānxīn	worry
12.	帮助	(V. & N.)	bāngzhù	help
13.	可是	(Conj.)	kěshì	but
14.	或者	(Conj.)	huòzhě	or
15.	有点儿	(Adv.)	yǒu diǎnr	a little; slightly
16.	别	(Adv.)	bié	don't (asking sb. not to do sth.)

Proper nouns

1.	四川	Sìchuān	a province of China
2.	云南	Yúnnán	a province of China

⚙ Listen to the dialogue and answer the following questions. (Try best to answer in Chinese.)

（1）Where is Jiang Shan going during the vacation? Will he go alone?

（2）When will Jiang Shan come back? How long will they travel?

（3）What is Jiang Shan worried about? How is Ding Hansheng's advice?

⚙ Listen to the recording while reading the text on the right. ⇨

⚙ Read aloud the text and try not to look at the pinyin.

⚙ Work in groups and act out the conversation.

⚙ Activity: Talk about your vacation plans with each other.

Vocabulary extension

明年	míngnián	next year	去年	qùnián	last year
后年	hòunián	the year after next	前年	qiánnián	the year before last
麻烦	máfan	trouble; troublesome	方便	fāngbiàn	convenient
安全	ānquán	safe; safety	危险	wēixiǎn	dangerous; danger
不要	búyào	don't（＝别）	不用	búyòng	needn't
放心	fàngxīn	put one's mind at ease; feel relieved			

_____

_____

Text

Ding Hansheng and Jiang Shan are chatting. Jiang Shan is going to travel to China with his girlfriend.

Dīng Hànshēng: Nǐmen shénme shíhou fàngjià?
丁　汉生：你们 什么 时候 放假？

Jiāng Shān: Sì yuè xiàxún.
江　山：四月 下旬。

Dīng Hànshēng: Fàngjià yǐhòu nǐ dǎsuàn gàn shénme?
丁　汉生：放假 以后 你 打算 干什么？

Jiāng Shān: Wǒ xiǎng qù Zhōngguó lǚxíng.
江　山：我 想 去 中国 旅行。

Dīng Hànshēng: Yào qù hěn duō dìfang ba?
丁　汉生：要 去 很多 地方 吧？

Jiāng Shān: Shì a, Běijīng, Shànghǎi, Sìchuān, Yúnnán …
江　山：是 啊，北京、上海、四川、云南……

Dīng Hànshēng: Shénme shíhou qù?
丁　汉生：什么 时候 去？

Jiāng Shān: Wǔ yuè shàngxún huòzhě zhōngxún.
江　山：五月 上旬 或者 中旬。

Dīng Hànshēng: Shénme shíhou huílái?
丁　汉生：什么 时候 回来？

Jiāng Shān: Wǒ dǎsuàn qī yuè yī hào yǐqián huílái.
江　山：我 打算七月一号以前回来。

Dīng Hànshēng: Nǐ yí gè rén qù ma?
丁　汉生：你一个人去吗？

Jiāng Shān: Bù, gēn wǒ de nǚ péngyou yìqǐ qù. Kěshì, wǒmen de Hànyǔ
江　山：不，跟我的女朋友一起去。可是，我们的汉语

bú tài hǎo, wǒ yǒu diǎnr dānxīn.
不太好，我有点儿担心。

Dīng Hànshēng: Nǐ bié dānxīn. Wǒ zài Běijīng, Shànghǎi, Sìchuān dōu yǒu péngyou,
丁　汉生：你别担心。我在北京、上海、四川都有 朋友，

kěyǐ qǐng tāmen bāngzhù nǐ.
可以请他们帮助你。

7.2

Tā Shòushòu De, Gāogāo De

她 瘦瘦 的，高高 的

She is thin and tall

Preliminary exercises

1 **Warm up**

(1) How do you say "come in, come out, go in, go out" in Chinese?

(2) Describe a person's features and ask everyone to guess who he/she is.

2 **Learn the following words and form correct sentences with the words under the teacher's guidance.**

（1）我们　刚　回来

（2）我　王老师　找　要

（3）这儿　没有　王老师

（4）你　来　看看　吧　一会儿　过　再

（5）她　眼镜　牛仔裤　一条　一副　穿　戴

3 **Listen to the recording twice. Try to repeat what you have heard with the hint of the following words.**

王老师是 _____。她 _____ 的，_____ 的，头发 _____ 的，皮肤 _____ 的，戴一副 _____，穿一件 _____，一条 _____。

Discussion:

If the adjectives 高，瘦，长 are reduplicated, what tone do you think they express?

Listening script

3 王老师她是瘦瘦的，她高高的，瘦瘦的，头发长长的，皮肤白白的，戴一副眼镜，穿一件红毛衣，一条牛仔裤。

Words and expressions

1.	找	(V.)	zhǎo	look for; want to see
2.	穿	(V.)	chuān	wear
3.	牛仔裤	(N.)	niúzǎikù	jeans
4.	戴	(V.)	dài	wear (a pair of glasses/a tie/ a watch…)
5.	眼镜	(N.)	yǎnjìng	glasses, spectacles
6.	副	(MW)	fù	a measure word for spectacles, gloves, etc.
7.	头发	(N.)	tóufa	hair
8.	长	(Adj.)	cháng	long
9.	瘦	(Adj.)	shòu	thin, emaciated, lean
10.	高	(Adj.)	gāo	tall, high
11.	皮肤	(N.)	pífū	skin
12.	出去	(DV)	chūqù	go out
	出	(DV)	chū	come/go out
13.	进来	(DV)	jìnlái	come in
14.	过	(DV)	guò	cross, pass, past
15.	一会儿		yíhuìr	a short while
16.	每	(Pron.)	měi	every
17.	刚	(Adv.)	gāng	only a short time ago; just
18.	再	(Adv.)	zài	again
19.	哦	(Interj.)	ò	oh

⚙ Listen to the dialogue and answer the following questions. (Try best to answer in Chinese.)

（1）Who is Jack looking for?

（2）What does the person whom Jack is looking for look like?

（3）What is the name of the person whom Jack is looking for? Is she in the office?

⚙ Listen to the recording while reading the text on the right. ⇨

⚙ Read aloud the text and try not to look at the pinyin.

⚙ Work in groups and act out the conversation.

⚙ Activity: A chooses a picture from the following and describes it to B. B judges which picture it is. B is allowed to ask questions if he/she doesn't quite understand A's description.

Vocabulary extension

样儿 / 样子	yàngr /yàngzi	appearance, manner	胖	pàng	fat
年轻	niánqīng	young	短	duǎn	short (in length)
矮	ǎi	short (in height)	鼻子	bízi	nose
脸	liǎn	face	嘴巴	zuǐba	mouth
眼睛	yǎnjing	eye	T恤	T-xù	T-shirt
裙子	qúnzi	skirt			

_____   _____

_____   _____

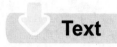 **Text**

Jack is now working and studying Chinese in Beijing. Today he is visiting his Chinese teacher, Miss Wang.)

Jiékè: Nǐ hǎo!   Kěyǐ   jìnlái   ma?
杰 克：你好！可以进来吗？

Lǎoshī: Nǐ zhǎo shuí?
老 师：你找谁？

Jiékè: Wǒ zhǎo Wáng lǎoshī.
杰 克：我找王老师。

Lǎoshī: Nǎ wèi Wáng lǎoshī?   Zhèr   yǒu liǎng wèi Wáng lǎoshī.
老 师：哪位王老师？这儿有两位王老师。

Jiékè: Wǒ bù zhīdào tā jiào shénme míngzi.   Tā shì nǚ de.
杰 克：我不知道她叫什么名字。她是女的。

Lǎoshī: Zhèr   de lǎoshī dōu shì nǚ de.
老 师：这儿的老师都是女的。

Jiékè: Tā dài yí fù yǎnjìng.
杰 克：她戴一副眼镜。

Lǎoshī: Zhèr   měi wèi lǎoshī dōu dài yǎnjìng.
老 师：这儿每位老师都戴眼镜。

Jiékè: Tā shòushòu de,   gāogāo de,   chuān yì tiáo niúzǎikù.
杰 克：她瘦瘦的，高高的，穿一条牛仔裤。

Lǎoshī: Tóufa chángcháng de,   pífū   báibái de?
老 师：头发 长长 的，皮肤白白的？

Jiékè: Duì duì duì.
杰 克：对对对。

Lǎoshī: Ò,   nǐ yào zhǎo Wáng Huān lǎoshī,   tā gāng chūqù.
老 师：哦，你要找王欢老师，她刚出去。

Jiékè: Tā dàgài shénme shíhou huílái?
杰 克：她大概什么时候回来？

Lǎoshī: Bù zhīdào.   nǐ guò yíhuìr   zài lái kànkan ba.
老 师：不知道。你过一会儿再来看看吧。

7.3 Language Points

以后 and 以前

"（……）以后" means *after*…, "（……）以前" means *before*…

以前，我不会说汉语。	Yǐqián, wǒ bú huì shuō Hànyǔ.
我七点钟以前回来。	Wǒ qī diǎnzhōng yǐqián huílái.
来这儿以前，他在北京工作。	Lái zhèr yǐqián, tā zài Běijīng gōngzuò.

以后，我想去北京工作。	Yǐhòu, wǒ xiǎng qù Běijīng gōngzuò.
我七点钟以后回来。	Wǒ qī diǎnzhōng yǐhòu huílái.
来这儿以后，他在我们大学学习。	Lái zhèr yǐhòu, tā zài wǒmen dàxué xuéxí.

还是 and 或者

Both 还是 and 或者 mean "or", but 还是 is usually used in the questions, while 或者 is used in the statements.
Other examples:

你打算这个月去还是下个月去？
Nǐ dǎsuàn zhè ge yuè qù háishi xià ge yuè qù?
Will you go this month or next month?

我打算这个月去或者下个月去。
Wǒ dǎsuàn zhè ge yuè qù huòzhě xià ge yuè qù.
I will go this month or next month.

你要茶还是咖啡？
Nǐ yào chá háishi kāfēi?
Do you want tea or coffee?

茶或者咖啡都可以。
Chá huòzhě kāfēi dōu kěyǐ.
Either is fine.

有点儿 and 一点儿

Both 一点儿 and 有点儿 mean "a little", but 一点儿 usually modifies nouns denoting quantity, e.g.

我会说一点儿汉语。	Wǒ huì shuō yìdiǎnr Hànyǔ.
我要喝一点儿茶。	Wǒ yào hē yìdiǎnr chá.

While 有点儿 is an adverb which modifies adjectives or verbs denoting degree, e.g.

他今天有点儿不高兴。 　　Tā jīntiān yǒu diǎnr bù gāoxìng.

这件衬衫有点儿贵。 　　Zhè jiàn chènshān yǒu diǎnr guì.

✤ Expressions of time（II）

A. Year, Month and Day

年 nián year

| 1949 年 | 一九四九年 | yī jiǔ sì jiǔ nián |
| 2008 年 | 二〇〇八年 | èr líng líng bā nián |

月 yuè month

一月 yī yuè	二月 èr yuè	三月 sān yuè
四月 sì yuè	五月 wǔ yuè	六月 liù yuè
七月 qī yuè	八月 bā yuè	九月 jiǔ yuè
十月 shí yuè	十一月 shíyī yuè	十二月 shí'èr yuè

号 hào / 日 rì day

| 一号 yī hào | 二号 èr hào | 三号 sān hào …… |
| 三十号 sānshí hào | 三十一号 sānshíyī hào | |

In written style "日 rì" is used instead of "号 hào".

B. Word order in dates

2005 年 4 月 30 日 / 号
二〇〇五 年 四月 三十日 / 号
èr líng líng wǔ nián sì yuè sānshí rì / hào

二〇一二 年 十月 三十日 上午 九点 四十分
èr líng yī èr nián shí yuè sānshí rì shàngwǔ jiǔ diǎn sìshí fēn

✤ Directional Verbs

Directional verbs in Chinese include two groups, monosyllabic directional verbs and disyllabic directional verbs, as follows:

进	出	上	下	过	回	来
jìn	chū	shàng	xià	guò	huí	lái
进来	出来	上来	下来	过来	回来	去
jìnlái	chūlái	shànglái	xiàlái	guòlái	huílái	qù
进去	出去	上去	下去	过去	回去	
jìnqù	chūqù	shàngqù	xiàqù	guòqù	huíqù	

Un
7

1. 进来吧！

2. 进去吧！

3. 出来吧！

4. 出去吧！

5. 上来吧！

6. 上去吧！

7. 下来吧！

8. 下去吧！

9. 过来吧！

10. 过去吧！

请进！　Qǐng jìn!

进来吧。Jìnlái ba.

你什么时候回来？　Nǐ shénme shíhou huílái?

Note: An object denoting location can't follow a disyllabic directional verb. It should be inserted between the two syllables of the verb, e.g.

我今天晚上不回学校去。　Wǒ jīntiān wǎnshang bù huí xuéxiào qù.

我们上山去吧。　Wǒmen shàng shān qù ba.

Unit
7

❖ The reduplication of adjectives

Some adjectives can be reduplicated. The reduplicated form of monosyllabic adjectives is AA as in 大大 dàdà, 红红 hónghóng; the reduplicated form of disyllabic adjectives is AABB in which the second syllable is pronounced lightly as in 漂漂亮亮 piàopiàoliàngliàng, 高高兴兴 gāogāoxìngxìng. In this case, reduplication is usd to intensify the adjective and suggest description.

The reduplicated form of adjectives is usually followed by "的 de" when they function as predicates or attributives.

她瘦瘦的，高高的，头发长长的。

Tā shòushòu de, gāogāo de, tóufa chángcháng de.

他们都高高兴兴的，你为什么不高兴？

Tāmen dōu gāogāoxìngxìng de, nǐ wèi shénme bù gāoxìng?

❖ Review exercises: Choose the correct sentences.

（1） A. 他明天回去英国。
B. 他明天回英国。
C. 他回英国明天。

（2） A. 那儿的东西有点儿贵。
B. 那儿的东西一点儿贵。
C. 那儿的东西一点儿太贵。

（3） A. 她瘦，高，白。
B. 她瘦瘦，高高，白白。
C. 她瘦瘦的，高高的，白白的。

（4） A. 他们五号七月放假。
B. 他们七月五号放假。
C. 他们放假七月五号。

（5） A. 你喜欢喝茶和喝咖啡吗？
B. 你喜欢喝茶或者喝咖啡？
C. 你喜欢喝茶还是喝咖啡？

（6） A. 下课以后你回家吗？
B. 以后下课你回家吗？
C. 下课以后你回去家吗？

文化点　Wénhuà Diǎn　Cultural notes

❖ There are two kinds of Chinese calendars: the official calendar, also known as the solar calendar (identical with the Gregorian calendar first used by Western countries), gōnglì or yánglì, and the lunar calendar (also known as the agrarian calendar), nónglì or yīnlì. The lunar calendar is based on the traditional Chinese calendric system which is calculated according to the moon's revolution around the earth in approximately 29.5 days. In the lunar system, a "greater month" consists of 30 days and a "smaller month" consists of 29 days. There are 12 lunar months in an ordinary lunar year, but since there are only 354 to 355 days a year in this system, sometimes extra "intercalary" months are added to make up for the lost time and keep the calendar in step with the seasons.

The principal traditional Chinese festivals are:

Spring Festival, 春节 Chūnjié: known in the West as Chinese New Year.

Lantern Festival, 元宵节 Yuánxiāojié: the fifteenth day of the first lunar month.

Tomb Sweeping Day, 清明节 Qīngmíngjié: one of the twenty-four solar periods; around the fifth of the fourth solar month.

Dragon Boat Festival, 端午节 Duānwǔjié: the fifth day of the fifth lunar month.

Mid-autumn Festival, 中秋节 Zhōngqiūjié: the fifteenth day of the eighth lunar month.

Double Ninth Festival, 重阳节 Chóngyángjié: the ninth day of the ninth lunar month.

The dates of other official holidays in China are calculated according to the solar Gregorian calendar:
New Year's Day, 元旦 Yuándàn: January 1st.
Women's Day, 妇女节 Fùnǚjié: March 8th.
Labor Day, 劳动节 Láodòngjié: May 1st.
Youth Day, 青年节 Qīngniánjié: May 4th.
Children's Day, 儿童节 Értóngjié: June 1st.
National Day, 国庆节 Guóqìngjié: October 1st.

The following are some Western festivals also celebrated in China.

Christmas   Shèngdànjié

Valentine's Day   Qíngrénjié

Easter   Fùhuójié

Thanksgiving   Gǎn'ēnjié

❀ In the eyes of most Chinese people, a fair-skinned female is beautiful. Thus skin-whitening products are an important part in the cosmetics market in China. In summer, you can see many females walking in the sun with an umbrella just to avoid being tanned.

❀ China now has a nine-year compulsory education system; that is, every child is expected to complete at least three years of junior high school education after six years of elementary school (xiǎoxué). After graduating from junior high school, students generally go on to senior high school or a vocational school. The six-year high school (zhōngxué) system consists of three years of junior high (chūzhōng), and three years of senior high school (gāozhōng). After graduating from high school and passing the higher education entrance examination (gāokǎo), some students will be able to attend university. An undergraduate degree program generally takes four years to complete. After graduation, most people start to work, but some go on to become graduate students (yánjiūshēng). Those who qualify for graduate school normally study three more years. After they successfully defend their theses, they are awarded a master's degree (shuòshì). There are also some who study another three or more years to gain a Ph.D. degree (bóshì).

❀ Aside from a small number of students whose homes are close to the university campus, making it convenient for them to live at home, most Chinese university students live in dormitories or student apartments, and they eat in the university's cafeterias (shítáng). Foreign students generally stay in the university's foreign student residences, but they can also rent rooms off campus. Some foreign students study together with Chinese students in different departments, but many study Chinese in a special department, which may be called the "International Cultural Exchange School", "Institute for Overseas Education" or "Center for Chinese Teaching".

❀ Chinese universities use a credit system. There are two semesters in each school year. The first semester runs from early September to just before the Spring Festival, generally in January of the next year. The second semester starts after the Spring Festival, generally in February and ends in early July. Each class is 45 to 50 minutes long, with a 10-minute break between classes.

Unit 8

Fùjìn Yǒu Méiyǒu Yínháng?
附近 有 没有 银行?
Is There a Bank Nearby?

Learning objectives

* Asking the way
* Identifying direction
* Identifying location

Key sentences

Fùjìn yǒu méiyǒu yínháng?
附近有 没有 银行?

Is there a bank nearby?

Yóujú jiù zài nà ge yínháng de pángbiān.
邮局 就 在 那 个 银行 的 旁边。

The post office is just beside the bank.

Wǎng qián zǒu, wǎng yòu guǎi.
往 前 走, 往 右 拐。

Go ahead, and turn right.

Dìtiě zhàn lí qìchē zhàn yuǎn bu yuǎn?
地铁 站 离 汽车 站 远 不 远?

Is the subway station far away from the bus stop?

Néng bu néng qí zìxíngchē qù?
能 不 能 骑 自行车 去?

Can I go there by bike?

8.1

往 前 走，往 右 拐

Go ahead, and turn right

Preliminary exercises

1 Warm up

(1) Can you ask directions in Chinese?

(2) Draw a simple map and decide a starting point. One student gives instructions, like 往前走，往左拐 , and 往右拐 , and asks the other to find the destination.

2 Learn the following words and form correct sentences with the words under the teacher's guidance.

（1）一个 邮局 有 附近

（2）往 往 前 左 走 拐

（3）中国 银行 怎么 去 走

（4）学校 你 家 离 远 不 远

（5）书店 咖啡馆 旁边 的 在 就

3 Learn the following words and choose the correct answer to fill in the blanks according to the recording.

过 就 离 条 怎么

（1）中国银行 _____ 这儿不太远。

（2）请问，_____ 去你的公司？

（3）_____ 两 _____ 马路，前面 _____ 有一个中国饭店。

4 Choose either 有 or 在 to fill in the blanks according to the recording.

（1）银行旁边 _____ 一个邮局。　　（2）邮局 _____ 银行旁边。

（3）我家附近 _____ 一个咖啡馆　　（4）咖啡馆 _____ 我家附近。

Discussion:

When should 有 be used and when should 在 be used?

1.	前面（前边）	（LW）	qiánmiàn(qiánbian)	front
2.	后面（后边）	（LW）	hòumiàn(hòubian)	behind
3.	左面（左边）	（LW）	zuǒmiàn(zuǒbian)	left
4.	右面（右边）	（LW）	yòumiàn(yòubian)	right
5.	上面（上边）	（LW）	shàngmiàn(shàngbian)	above, on
6.	下面（下边）	（LW）	xiàmiàn(xiàbian)	below, under
7.	里面（里边）	（LW）	lǐmiàn(lǐbian)	in, inside
8.	外面（外边）	（LW）	wàimiàn(wàibian)	outside
9.	附近	（LW）	fùjìn	nearby
10.	旁边	（LW）	pángbiān	beside
11.	银行	（N.）	yínháng	bank
12.	邮局	（N.）	yóujú	post office
13.	马路	（N.）	mǎlù	road
	路	（N.）	lù	road, route
14.	行人	（N.）	xíngrén	pedestrian
15.	走	（V.）	zǒu	go, walk, leave
16.	拐	（V.）	guǎi	turn
17.	远	（Adj.）	yuǎn	far
18.	近	（Adj.）	jìn	near
19.	离	（Prep.）	lí	away from
20.	往	（Prep.）	wǎng	toward
21.	怎么	（Adv.）	zěnme	how
22.	就	（Adv.）	jiù	just (for emphasis)
23.	不客气		bú kèqi	You're welcome. (answer for 谢谢)
	客气	（Adj.）	kèqi	polite, courteous, modest

Un
8

✿ Listen to the dialogue and answer the following questions. (Try best to answer in Chinese.)
   （1）Where are Jiang Shan and his girlfriend going? Do they know the way?
   （2）Are the bank and the post office far away from their living place?
   （3）How can they get to the bank and the post office?

✿ Listen to the recording while reading the text on the right. ⇨

✿ Read aloud the text and try not to look at the pinyin.

✿ Work in groups and act out the conversation.

✿ Activity: Talk about the places around your campus and how to get there.

Vocabulary extension

东面 （东边）	dōngmiàn (dōngbian)	east	南面 （南边）	nánmiàn (nánbian)	south
西面 （西边）	xīmiàn (xīmiàn)	west	北面 （北边）	běimiàn (běibian)	north
对面	duìmiàn	opposite	中间	zhōngjiān	center, middle
食堂	shítáng	canteen, cafeteria	图书馆	túshūguǎn	library
教学楼	jiàoxuélóu	teaching building	花园	huāyuán	garden

Text

Jiang Shan and his girlfriend are traveling in China. After they arrive in the city they look for a bank and a post office.

Jiāng Shān:　Qǐngwèn,　fùjìn　yǒu méiyǒu yínháng?
江　山：请问，附近有 没有 银行？

Xíngrén:　Yǒu。Fùjìn　yǒu yí gè Zhōngguó Yínháng.
行　人：有。附近有一个 中国 银行。

Jiāng Shān:　Lí　zhèr yuǎn bu yuǎn?
江　山：离这儿远不 远？

Xíngrén:　Bú tài yuǎn.
行　人：不太远。

Jiāng Shān:　Zěnme zǒu?
江　山：怎么走？

Xíngrén:　wǎng qián zǒu　yìdiǎnr,　wǎng yòu guǎi,　guò liǎng tiáo mǎlù,　jiù shì
行　人：往 前走一点儿，往 右拐，过 两 条马路，就是

Zhōngguó Yínháng.
中国　银行。

Jiāng Shān:　Fùjìn　yǒu méiyǒu yóujú?
江　山：附近有 没有 邮局？

Xíngrén:　Yǒu。Yóujú　jiù zài nà ge　yínháng de pángbiān.
行　人：有。邮局就在那个银行 的旁边。

Jiāng Shān:　Xièxie nín!
江　山：谢谢您！

Xíngrén:　Bú kèqi.
行　人：不客气。

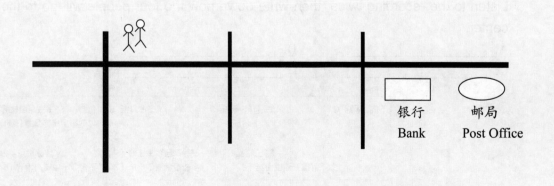

8.2

Wǒmen Kěyǐ Zuò Dìtiě Qù

我们 可以 坐 地铁去

We can get there by subway

Preliminary exercises

1 Warm up:

(1) Which do you prefer, cycling, driving, or riding a bus?

(2) As you know, how is the traffic situation in the big cities of China?

2 Learn the following words and form correct sentences with the words under the teacher's guidance.

（1）学校　门口　地铁站　在　就

（2）这儿　市中心　不太　远　从　到

（3）自行车　学校　骑　去　每天　我

（4）坐　公共汽车　换　地铁　先　然后

（5）我们　去　去　还是　打　车　坐　公共汽车

3 Learn the following words and choose the correct answer to fill in the blanks according to the recording.

从　离　到　上　下

（1）＿＿＿＿学校＿＿＿＿市中心很近。　　（2）市中心＿＿＿＿学校很近。

（3）我不知道在哪儿＿＿＿＿车。　　（4）车＿＿＿＿有很多老人。

（5）你＿＿＿＿车以后往前走一点儿，就＿＿＿＿了。

Questions:

What is the difference between 从 and 离？Do 车上 and 上车 mean the same?

4 Listen to the recording twice, then write down how the four people will go to the city center.

A:＿＿＿＿＿＿＿＿＿＿＿＿＿。　　B:＿＿＿＿＿＿＿＿＿＿＿＿＿。

C:＿＿＿＿＿＿＿＿＿＿＿＿＿。　　D:＿＿＿＿＿＿＿＿＿＿＿＿＿。

Words and expressions

1.	公共汽车		gōnggòng qìchē	bus
	汽车	(N.)	qìchē	automobile; motor vehicle
	车	(N.)	chē	vehicle
2.	地铁	(N.)	dìtiě	subway, metro, underground, tube
3.	站	(N.)	zhàn	station, stop
4.	坐	(V.)	zuò	take (vehicle, subway, train, plane, etc.)
5.	自行车	(N.)	zìxíngchē	bicycle
6.	市中心		shì zhōngxīn	downtown
	市	(N.)	shì	city
	中心	(N.)	zhōngxīn	center
7.	门口	(PW)	ménkǒu	gate, doorway
8.	骑	(V.)	qí	ride
9.	打车		dǎchē	take the taxi; (go) by taxi
10.	从	(Prep.)	cóng	from
11.	到	(Prep. &V.)	dào	to, until; arrive
12.	换	(V.)	huàn	change
13.	上车		shàng chē	get on
14.	下车		xià chē	get off
15.	告诉	(V.)	gàosu	tell
16.	先	(Adv.)	xiān	first
17.	然后	(Conj.)	ránhòu	then

🔧 Listen to the dialogue and answer the following questions. (Try best to answer in Chinese.)

（1）Where are Jiang Shan and his girlfriend going?

（2）Is the downtown far away from where they are now?

（3）How can they get to the downtown?

（4）How can they get to the subway station from the bus station?

🔧 Listen to the recording while reading the text on the right. ⇨

🔧 Read aloud the text and try not to look at the pinyin.

🔧 Work in groups and act out the conversation.

🔧 Activity: Talk about how you get to school/work every day and how do you get there if you take public transportation.

Vocabulary extension

火车	huǒchē	train		飞机	fēijī	plane
船	chuán	ship, boat		开（车）	kāi (chē)	to drive
出租汽车	chūzū qìchē	taxi		打的	dǎdí	take taxi; (go) by taxi
走路	zǒulù	to walk; go on foot				
辆	liàng	a measure word for vehicles				

_____   _____

_____   _____

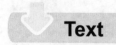 **Text**

Jiang Shan and Zhang Yuanyuan are talking about how to go downtown from a university campus.

> 打车 dǎchē, also 打的 dǎdí, means "take a taxi".

Jiāng Shān: Wǒmen xiànzài dǎchē qù shì zhōngxīn ma?

江　山：我们现在打车去市中心吗?

Zhāng Yuányuan: Yǒu rén gàosu wǒ, kěyǐ zuò dìtiě qù.

张　园园：有人告诉我，可以坐地铁去。

Jiāng Shān: Nǐ zhīdào zěnme zǒu ma?
江　山：你知道怎么走吗？

Zhāng Yuányuan: Bù zhīdào.
张　园园：不知道。

Jiāng Shān: Wǒmen wèn yíxià ba.
江　山：我们问一下吧。

(to a college student passing by)

Zhāng Yuányuan: Tóngxué, qǐngwèn cóng zhèr dào shì zhōngxīn zěnme zǒu?
张　园园：同学，请问从这儿到市中心怎么走？

Xuésheng: Nǐ zài xuéxiào ménkǒu zuò yāo sān jiǔ lù gōnggòng qìchē, zuò wǔ zhàn,
学　生：你在学校门口坐１３９路公共汽车，坐五站，

ránhòu huàn dìtiě, zuò liǎng zhàn, cóng dìtiě zhàn chūlái, jiù shì
然后换地铁，坐两站，从地铁站出来，就是

shì zhōngxīn.
市中心。

Zhāng Yuányuan: Dìtiě zhàn lí qìchē zhàn yuǎn bu yuǎn?
张　园园：地铁站离汽车站远不远？

Xuésheng: Bù yuǎn. Nǐ xià chē yǐhòu wǎng yòu guǎi, guò mǎlù, jiù shì
学　生：不远。你下车以后往右拐，过马路，就是

dìtiě zhàn.
地铁站。

Jiāng Shān: Néng bu néng qí zìxíngchē qù?
江　山：能不能骑自行车去？

Xuésheng: Bù xíng, tài yuǎn le.
学　生：不行，太远了。

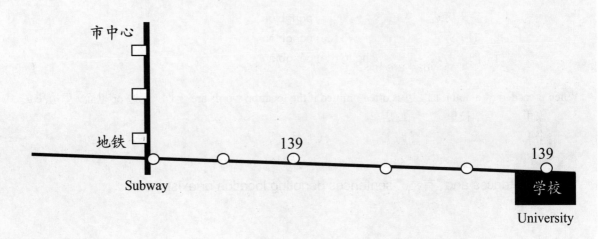

8.3   Language Points

❧ Location words and place expressions

The Chinese location words are as follows:

前	后	左	右	上	下	里	外	……
qián	hòu	zuǒ	yòu	shàng	xià	lǐ	wài	…

前面	后面	左面	右面	上面	下面	里面	外面	……
qiánmiàn	hòumiàn	zuǒmiàn	yòumiàn	shàngmiàn	xiàmiàn	lǐmiàn	wàimiàn	…

前边	后边	左边	右边	上边	下边	里边	外边	……
qiánbian	hòubian	zuǒbian	yòumian	shàngbian	xiàbian	lǐbian	wàibian	…

And:

附近	旁边	……
fùjìn	pángbiān	…

A disyllabic location word or a noun/pronoun followed by a location word indicates a specific place.

> ### (P. / N. +) LW
>
> | 前面 | qiánmiàn |
> |---|---|
> | 我（的）前面 | wǒ (de) qiánmiàn |
> | 银行（的）前面 | yínháng (de) qiánmiàn |
>
> | 旁边 | pángbiān |
> |---|---|
> | 我（的）旁边 | wǒ (de) pángbiān |
> | 银行（的）旁边 | yínháng (de) pángbiān |

When preceded by a noun, 面 / 边 is often omitted if the location words are 上面 / 上边 or 里面 / 里边, e.g.

家里　　　学校里　　　商店里

书上　　　天上　　　路上　　　汽车上

❧ "在zài" sentences and "有yǒu" sentences denoting location or existence

Sth./Sb. (definite) + 在 + a place

Somebody or something is in/on/at…

我在英国。 Wǒ zài Yīngguó.

那个邮局在银行旁边。 Nà ge yóujú zài yínháng pángbiān.

江山的词典在桌子上。 Jiāng Shān de cídiǎn zài zhuōzi shang.

A place + 有 + sth./sb. (indefinite)

There is something or somebody in/at/on…

我家有五口人。 Wǒ jiā yǒu wǔ kǒu rén.

附近有一个中国银行。 Fùjìn yǒu yí gè Zhōngguó Yínháng.

银行里有很多人。 Yínháng li yǒu hěn duō rén.

✤ Review exercises: Choose the correct sentences.

（1） A. 你知道怎么走吗?
　　　 B. 你知道什么走吗?
　　　 C. 你知道怎么走呢?

（2） A. 这儿从地铁站有点儿远。
　　　 B. 这儿离地铁站有点儿远。
　　　 C. 这儿离地铁站一点儿远。

（3） A. 往左拐以后下车。
　　　 B. 以后下车往左拐。
　　　 C. 下车以后往左拐。

（4） A. 附近有那个中国银行。
　　　 B. 附近有一个中国银行。
　　　 C. 附近在一个中国银行。

（5） A. 那个商店就在旁边我家。
　　　 B. 我家旁边就在那个商店。
　　　 C. 那个商店就在我家旁边。

（6） A. 我打算骑自行车去。
　　　 B. 我打算坐自行车去。
　　　 C. 我打算去自行车。

文化点　Wénhuà Diǎn　Cultural notes

✤ In China, the first choice of most people for long distance travel is the train (huǒchē). Naturally, many people also choose airplanes (fēijī) or long distance buses (chángtú qìchē). The commonest modes of transportation in large cities are public buses (gōnggòng qìchē) and the subway (dìtiě).

✤ Private cars have become very common in many Chinese cities. Due to the increase of cars, traffic in big cities is becoming heavier. However, bicycles (zìxíngchē) and scooters (diàndòngchē) are quite commonly used.

English Translation of the Texts

Unit 1

1.1 What's your name?

Bai Xiaohong:	Hello.
Wang Ying:	Hello.
Martin:	Hello.
Wang Ying:	(to Bai Xiaohong) What's your name?
Bai Xiaohong:	My name is Bai Xiaohong. What about you two?
Wang Ying:	My name is Wang Ying.
Martin:	I'm Martin.
Wang Ying:	(to Bai Xiaohong) Where are you from?
Bai Xiaohong:	I'm Chinese. And you?
Wang Ying:	I am Canadian.
Bai Xiaohong:	(to Martin) Are you also Canadian?
Martin:	No, I am not Canadian. I'm Australian.

1.2 What's your surname?

Students:	Hello, teacher.
Mr. Zhang:	Hello, students.
Martin:	Sir, what is your surname?
Mr. Zhang:	My surname is Zhang. My name is Zhang Lin. What's your name?
Martin:	My name is Martin.
Mr. Zhang:	What is your nationality?
Martin:	I'm Australian.
Mr. Zhang:	(to Jiang Shan) How about you?
Jiang Shan:	My name is Jiang Shan. I'm American.
Mr. Zhang:	(to Wang Ying) Are you also American?
Wang Ying:	No, I'm not American. I'm Canadian.
Mr. Zhang:	Do you speak English or French?
Wang Ying:	I speak English. We all speak English. Do you speak English, Mr. Zhang?
Mr. Zhang:	I don't speak English. I only speak Chinese.

Unit 2

2.1 I work in an import and export corporation

Jack:	Hello.
Ding Hansheng:	Hello.
Jack:	I work in an import and export corportation.
Ding Hansheng:	Me too. (exchanging name cards)
Jack:	Glad to meet you.
Ding Hansheng:	Glad to meet you too. You speak good Chinese.
Jack:	Thanks. We both work in import and export companies….
Ding Hansheng:	We could have some sort of cooperation.
Jack:	Of course we can.
Ding Hansheng:	You may call or email me.
Jack:	OK.

2.2 Eastern College is big and beautiful

Jiang Shan:	This is my girlfriend, Zhang Yuanyuan.
Ding Hansheng:	Come in, please.
Zhang Yuanyuan:	Thank you.
Ding Hansheng:	Sit down, please.
Jiang Shan:	Thank you.
Ding Hansheng:	Would you like a cup of tea?
Zhang Yuanyuan:	Yes, thank you.
Ding Hansheng:	Where do you study?
Zhang Yuanyuan:	I study at the Dept. of Chinese Language, Eastern College in the U. K.
Ding Hansheng:	Oh! What do you think of that college?
Zhang Yuanyuan:	Very nice. It is very big and beautiful. I like it very much.

Unit 3

3.1 The child is cute

Bai Xiaohong:	Where are you from?
Ding Hansheng:	I'm from Guangdong Province. What about you?
Bai Xiaohonmg:	I'm from Guangdong Province, too.
Ding Hansheng:	Are you alone here?
Bai Xiaohong:	Yes, I am. How about you?
Ding Hansheng:	My family is here.
Bai Xiaohong:	How many people are there in your family?
Ding Hansheng:	There are five: father, mother, my wife and I, and a child.
Bai Xiaohong:	A boy or a girl?

Ding Hansheng:	A girl.
Bai Xiaohong:	How old is she?
Ding Hansheng:	Two.
Bai Xiaohong:	She must be very cute.
Ding Hansheng:	Yes, very cute.

3.2 How many students are there in your university?

Jack:	How many students are there in your university?
Zhang Lin:	I think there are about thirty thousand students.
Jack:	Are there any students studying Chinese?
Zhang Lin:	There are many students studying Chinese.
Jack:	About how many?
Zhang Lin:	A thousand or so.
Jack:	I want to study Chinese at your university, too.
Zhang Lin:	Why do you want to study Chinese?
Jack:	We have a branch company in China. My boss wants me to work there.

Unit 4

4.1 Do you want the Chinese one or the English one?

Jiang Shan:	Do you have a map of China?
Bai Xiaohong:	Yes, I have two. One is in Chinese, the other is in English.
Jiang Shan:	May I have a look?
Bai Xiaohong:	Yes, of course. Do you want the Chinese one or the English one?
Jiang Shan:	I want the English one.
Bai Xiaohong:	Here you are. This map is in English.
Jiang Shan:	Thank you.
Bai Xiaohong:	Why do you want to look at the map of China? You are planning to go to China, aren't you?
Jiang Shan:	Yes, I want to take a trip to China.
Bai Xiaohong:	Good! (unfolding the map) Look. This is Beijing.
Jiang Shan:	I know.
Bai Xiaohong:	This is Shanghai.
Jiang Shan:	I know.
Bai Xiaohong:	This is Longshan.
Jiang Shan:	Longshan? I don't know it. Is it a big place?
Bai Xiaohong:	No. It's small. My home is there.
Jiang Shan:	This name is really interesting! Are there any dragons there?
Bai Xiaohong:	No dragons. Only mountains.

4.2 This dictionary is very useful

Martin:	What dictionary is this?
Jiang Shan:	It's a Chinese-English dictionary.
Martin:	What about that one?
Jiang Shan:	An English-Chinese dictionary.
Martin:	Are these two dictionaries yours?
Jiang Shan:	This Chinese-English dictionary is mine but that English-Chinese dictionary is not mine.
Martin:	Whose dictionary is it?
Jinag Shan:	I have no idea. I think it may be the teacher's.

(At this moment the teacher Mr. Zhang enters the classroom.)

Martin:	Excuse me, Mr. Zhang. Is this your dictionary?
Mr. Zhang:	Yes, it's mine.
Martin:	What do you think of this dictionary?
Mr. Zhang:	It's very good and very useful.
Martin:	May I borrow it?
Mr. Zhang:	Of course.

Unit 5

5.1 How much is this white shirt?

Jack:	Ni hao!
Saleswoman:	Oh, you can speak Chinese!
Jack:	Yes, I can speak a little.
Saleswoman:	What do you want?
Jack:	I want to buy a shirt. How much is this white shirt?
Saleswoman:	Four hundred and twenty eight yuan.
Jack:	It's too expensive. Can it be cheaper?
Saleswoman:	No. That red one is cheaper, a hundred and sixty-five yuan. It looks better.
Jack:	All right. I'll take that one.
Saleswoman:	What else do you want?
Jack:	A pair of pants. May I try them on?
Saleswoman:	Of course.

… …

Saleswoman:	How do you like them?
Jack:	They are too big.
Saleswoman:	Then try on these. They aren't too big.

5.2 What's the most delicious dish?

Waitress:	Please take your seat. Have a cup of tea.

Martin, Jiang Shan, Bai Xiaohong, Wang Ying:	Thank you.
Waitress:	What may I bring you?
Martin:	Miss, what's the most delicious dish in your restaurant?
Waitress:	Fish in sweet and sour sauce.
Martin:	OK. We want the fish in sweet and sour sauce.
Wang Ying:	I want vegetables.
Waitress:	OK. Would you like some beef?
Bai Xiaohong:	OK. Stewed beef.
Jiang Shan:	I like spicy food the most. (to others) Can you eat spicy food?
Wang Ying:	Yes, but only a little.
Jiang Shan:	(to the waitress) I want to order sour-and-hot soup.
Waitress:	What else do you want?
Bai Xiaohong:	Rice.
Martin:	Dumplings.
Waitress:	OK. Wait a minute, please.

Unit 6

6.1 I have an appointment tomorrow evening

Bai Xiaohong:	Tomorrow is Saturday. We won't have classes. What are you going to do?
Jiang Shan:	I'm going to work tomorrow.
Wang Ying:	I have an engagement tomorrow evening.
Bai Xiaoying:	What will you do during the day?
Wang Ying:	I'll stay at home and rest. How about you?
Bai Xiaohong:	I'm going to play a ball game. Will you go with me?
Martin:	I'll go with you.
Bai Xiaohong:	Great. Wang Ying, will you go?
Wang Ying:	No, I won't. I don't like playing ball games.
Bai Xiaohong:	Then, what do you like?
Wang Ying:	I like watching TV at home.

6.2 I would like to invite you for a cup of coffee

Bai Xiaohong:	Hello.
Martin:	Is that Xiaohong?
Bai Xiaohong:	Yes. Who is calling?
Martin:	This is Martin.
Bai Xiaohong:	Hi, Martin. What's up?
Martin:	I would like to invite you to have coffee together.
Bai xiaohong:	When?
Martin:	This evening. Is that OK?

Bai Xiaohong:	But I cannot have coffee with you this evening. I'm busy. I will go see a friend and have to do my homework. I'm sorry.
Martin:	That's all right. How about tomorrow evening?
Bai Xiaohong:	I am free tomorrow evening. What time?
Martin:	8:30 pm. OK?
Bai Xiaohong:	All right. Where shall we meet?
Martin:	Bright Moon Coffee Shop.
Bai Xiaohong:	That's good. See you tomorrow evening. Thank you.
Martin:	See you then.
Bai Xiaohong:	See you.

Unit 7

7.1 I'll come back before July 1st

Ding Hansheng:	When will you take your vacation?
Jiang Shan:	During the last ten days of April.
Ding Hansheng:	What are you going to do during the vacation?
Jiang Shan:	I'm going to travel to China.
Ding Hansheng:	You will go to many places, won't you?
Jiang Shan:	Yes, I'll go to Beijing, Shanghai, Sichuan, Yunnan....
Ding Hansheng:	When will you go?
Jiang Shan:	During early May or mid-May.
Ding Hansheng:	When will you come back?
Jiang Shan:	I'll come back before July 1st.
Ding Hansheng:	Will you go alone?
Jiang Shan:	No, I'll go with my girlfriend. But, our Chinese is poor. I am a little worried.
Ding Hansheng:	Don't worry. I have friends in Beijing, Shanghai and Sichuan. You can ask them for help.

7.2 She is thin and tall

Jack:	Excuse me. May I come in?
Teacher:	Who do you want to see?
Jack:	I want to see Teacher Wang.
Teacher:	Which one? There are two teachers named Wang here.
Jack:	I don't know her name. She is a female.
Teacher:	All the teachers here are females.
Jack:	She wears glasses.
Teacher:	All the teachers here wear glasses.
Jack:	She is thin and tall with long hair and wears a pair of jeans.

Teacher:	Oh. You mean Wang Huan. She has just gone out.
Jack:	When will she be back?
Teacher:	I don't know. Please come back in a little while.

Unit 8

8.1 Go ahead, and turn right

Jiang Shan:	Excuse me. Is there a bank nearby?
Pedestrian:	Yes, there is a Bank of China nearby.
Jiang Shan:	Is it far away or not?
Pedestrian:	It's not too far away.
Jiang Shan:	How can I get there?
Pedestrian:	Go ahead, then turn right, and go straight for two blocks. The bank is right there.
Jiang Shan:	Is there a post office nearby?
Pedestrian:	Yes, there is. The post office is just beside the bank.
Jiang Shan:	Thank you very much.
Pedestrian:	You are welcome.

8.2 We can get there by subway

Jiang Shan:	Now shall we take a taxi to the downtown?
Zhang Yuanyuan:	Someone told me that we can get there by subway.
Jiang Shan:	Do you know how to get there?
Zhang Yuanyuan:	No, I don't.
Jiang Shan:	Let's ask directions.

(to a college student passing by)

Zhang Yuanyuan:	Excuse me. How can we go downtown?
Student:	You can take the No.139 bus and get off at the fifth stop, then change to the subway and get off at the second stop. There you will be in downtown.
Zhang Yuanyuan:	Is the subway stop far away from the bus stop?
Student:	No, it isn't far. When you get off the bus, you turn right and cross the street and the subway stop is right there.
Jiang Shan:	Can we get there by bike?
Student:	No, you can't. It is too far.

Supplementary Text

Xióngmāo
熊　猫
Panda

Words and expressions

1.	熊猫	(N.)	xióngmāo	panda
2.	它	(Pron.)	tā	it
3.	耳朵	(N.)	ěrduo	ear
4.	眼睛	(N.)	yǎnjing	eye
5.	尾巴	(N.)	wěiba	tail
6.	短	(N.)	duǎn	short
7.	身体	(N.)	shēntǐ	body
8.	胖	(Adj.)	pàng	fat, plump
9.	爬	(V.)	pá	climb
10.	睡懒觉		shuì lǎnjiào	get up late
	睡觉		shuìjiào	sleep
	懒	(Adj.)	lǎn	lazy
11.	开夜车		kāi yèchē	work late (lit. "drive the night car")
	开	(V.)	kāi	drive
	夜	(N.)	yè	night
12.	竹子	(N.)	zhúzi	bamboo
13.	顿	(MW)	dùn	a measure word for meals
14.	汉堡包	(N.)	hànbǎobāo	hamburger
15.	生活	(N. & V.)	shēnghuó	life; live
16.	省	(N.)	shěng	province
17.	天	(MW & N.)	tiān	day, sky

Bái Xiǎohóng: Nǐ zhīdào xióngmāo ma?
白小红：你知道 熊猫 吗？

Mǎdīng: Dāngrán zhīdào.
马 丁：当然 知道。

Bái Xiǎohóng: Xióngmāo hěn kě'ài.
白小红： 熊猫 很可爱。

Mǎdīng: Xióngmāo shì wǒmen de hǎo péngyou.
马 丁：熊猫 是我们的好 朋友。

Bái Xiǎohóng: Tā ěrduo xiǎoxiǎo de.
白小红：它耳朵 小小 的。

Mǎdīng: Yǎnjing dàdà de.
马 丁：眼睛大大的。

Bái Xiǎohóng: Wěiba duǎnduǎn de.
白小红：尾巴 短短 的。

Mǎdīng: Shēntǐ pàngpàng de.
马 丁：身体 胖胖 的。

Bái Xiǎohóng: Měi tiān zǒulái zǒuqù, páshàng páxià.
白小红：每天走来走去，爬上 爬下。

Mǎdīng: Báitiān shuì lǎnjiào, wǎnshang kāi yèchē.
马 丁：白天 睡懒觉，晚上 开夜车。

Bái Xiǎohóng: Tā xǐhuan chī zhúzi.
白小红：它喜欢吃竹子。

Mǎdīng: Tā yí dùn néng chī sān gè hànbǎobāo.
马 丁：他一顿 能 吃三个汉堡包。

Bái Xiǎohóng: Tā shēnghuó zài Zhōngguó Sìchuān Shěng.
白小红：它生活在 中国 四川 省。

Mǎdīng: Tā měi tiān gēn wǒmen zài yìqǐ.
马 丁：他每天 跟我们在一起。

Bái Xiǎohóng: Nǐ shuō de shì Zhōngguó de dà xióngmāo?
白小红：你说 的是 中国 的大 熊猫？

Mǎdīng: Bù, wǒ shuō de shì wǒmen de yí wèi tóngxué, wǒmen dōu jiào tā "xióng māo".
马 丁：不，我说的是我们的一位同学，我们都叫他"熊猫"。

Two Chinese Folk Songs

Mài Tāngyuán
卖　汤圆
Selling Sweet Glutinous Rice Dumplings

台湾民歌

卖　汤　圆，　　　卖　汤　圆，　　小二哥的汤　圆是　圆　又　圆。
卖　汤　圆，　　　卖　汤　圆，　　小二哥的汤　圆是　圆　又　圆。
卖　汤　圆，　　　卖　汤　圆，　　小二哥的汤　圆是　圆　又　圆。

一　碗汤　圆　满　又　满，　　三　毛钱　呀　卖　一　碗。
一　碗汤　圆　满　又　满，　　三　毛钱　呀　卖　一　碗。
要　吃汤　圆　快　来　买，　　吃　了汤　圆　好　团　圆。

汤　圆汤　圆　卖　汤　圆，　　汤圆一样可　以　当　茶　饭。
汤　圆汤　圆　卖　汤　圆，　　公平交易可　以　保　退　换。
汤　圆汤　圆　卖　汤　圆，　　慢来一步只　怕　要　卖　完。

哎　　嘿　　哎　　嘿　　汤　圆　汤　圆　卖　汤　圆，
哎　　嘿　　哎　　嘿　　汤　圆　汤　圆　卖　汤　圆，
哎　　嘿　　哎　　嘿　　汤　圆　汤　圆　卖　汤　圆，

汤圆一样可 以　当　茶　饭。
公平交易可 以　保　退　换。
慢来一步只 怕　要　卖　完。

Selling Sweet Glutinous Rice Dumplings

Dumplings for sale! Dumplings for sale!

Xiao'erge's dumplings are really round, and a bowl of dumplings is full to the brim. At three *mao* a bowl, it is a fair deal. If you are not satisfied with the dumplings, you can take them back and exchange them. But if you want to eat dumplings, you'd better be quick to buy them. After eating the dumplings, you will be reunited with your family. But if you are one step too slow, I'm afraid they will sell out.

Notes:

汤圆 tāngyuán: These sweet dumplings are made from glutinous rice flour and are also called 元宵 yuánxiāo. Traditionally they are eaten during the Lantern Festival (the night of the 15th of the first lunar month). Nowadays they are available every season.

小二哥: In traditional society people called their young male helpers or vendors 小二哥 or 店小二.

团圆 tuányuán (reunion): As 汤圆 (tāngyuán) and 团圆 (tuányuán) sound similar, eating dumplings makes people think of reunion. The ancient Chinese people were good at this kind of association, particularly in the field of eating. For example, when celebrating their birthdays, people should eat noodles because noodles are long and imply longevity; on Mid-autumn Festival people eat moon cakes. The shape of the moon cake and the round moon imply reunion with family or friends. When they are married, people eat candies which imply the sweetness of their married life.

Kāngdìng Qínggē
康 定 情 歌
The Love Song of Kangding

跑马（溜溜的）山　　上　　　一朵（溜溜的）云（哟）！
李家（溜溜的）大　　姐　　　人才（溜溜的）好（哟）！
一来（溜溜的）看　　上　　　人才（溜溜的）好（哟）！
世间（溜溜的）女　　子　　　任我（溜溜的）爱（哟）！

端端（溜溜的）　照　在　　康 定（溜溜的）　城（哟）！
张家（溜溜的）　大　哥　　看 上（溜溜的）　她（哟）！
二来（溜溜的）　看　上　　会 当（溜溜的）　家（哟）！
世间（溜溜的）　男　子　　任 你（溜溜的）　求（哟）！

月亮　　弯　　弯　　康 定（溜 溜 的）　城（哟）！
月亮　　弯　　弯　　看 上（溜 溜 的）　她（哟）！
月亮　　弯　　弯　　会 当（溜 溜 的）　家（哟）！
月亮　　弯　　弯　　任 你（溜 溜 的）　求（哟）！

The Love Song of Kangding

Over Paoma Hill there is a cloud which illuminates Kangding Town. In Kangding Town, the daughter of the Li family was known to be a rare beauty, and the son of the Zhang family fell deeply in love with her because of her beauty and many talents. (The boy said to the girl) there are so many girls I like in the world who I can choose, and there are so many boys in the world you like who you can choose.

Notes:

康定 Kāngdìng: A small city located to the west of Chengdu（成都）and on the western highlands of Sichuan Province, where many Han and Tibetan Chinese live together. The Sichuan-Tibet Highway passes through this area, with Kangding acting as the gateway to Tibet, and a market town for the border regions of Sichuan and Gansu provinces.

跑马山 Pǎomǎ Shān or Horserace Hill: A famous tourist site almost 3000 meters above sea level. There is a broad pasture on top of the hill where Tibetans used to hold horse races, hence its name. Kangding lies at the foot of the hill.

词语索引 Index of Vocabulary

The number after each word represents the ordinal number of the unit.

93. 好 hǎo / 1.1

94. 好吃 hǎochī / 5.2

95. 好的 hǎo de / 2.1

96. 号（日）hào(rì) / 7.1

97. 号码 hàomǎ / 2.1

98. 喝 hē / 2.2

99. 合作 hézuò / 2.1

100. 和 hé / 3.1

101. 很 hěn / 2.1

102. 红 hóng / 5.1

103. 红烧 hóngshāo / 5.2

104. 后面（后边）hòumiàn
   (hòubian) / 8.1

105. 还 hái / 5.1

106. 还是 háishi / 1.2

107. 换 huàn / 8.2

108. 回 huí / 7.1

109. 回来 huílái / 7.1

110. 会 huì / 5.1

111. 或者 huòzhě / 7.1

112. 几 jǐ / 3.1

113. 家 jiā / 3.1

114. 家里 jiā li / 6.1

115. 见 jiàn / 6.2

116. 见面 jiànmiàn / 6.2

117. 件 jiàn / 5.1

118. 叫 jiào / 1.1

119. 教室 jiàoshì / 4.2

120. 她 tā / 1.1

121. 今年 jīnnián / 7.1

122. 今天 jīntiān / 6.1

123. 近 jìn / 8.1

124. 进 jìn / 2.2

125. 进出口 jìn-chūkǒu / 2.1

126. 进口 jìnkǒu / 2.1

127. 进来 jìnlái / 7.2

128. 九 jiǔ / 0

129. 就 jiù / 8.1

130. 咖啡 kāfēi / 6.2

131. 咖啡馆 kāfēiguǎn / 6.2

132. 看 kàn / 4.1

133. 看电视 kàn diànshì / 6.1

134. 可爱 kě'ài / 3.1

135. 可是 kěshì / 7.1

136. 可以 kěyǐ / 2.1

137. 刻 kè / 6.2

138. 客气 kèqi / 8.1

139. 空儿 kòngr / 6.2

140. 口 kǒu / 3.1

141. 裤子 kùzi / 5.1

142. 块（元）kuài (yuán) / 5.1

143. 辣 là / 5.2

144. 来 lái / 3.2

145. 老板 lǎobǎn / 3.2

146. 老师 lǎoshī / 1.2

147. 离 lí / 8.1

148. 里 lǐ / 6.1

149. 里面（里边）lǐmiàn
   (lǐbian) / 8.1

150. 两 liǎng / 3.1

151. ○（零）líng / 2.1

152. 六 liù / 0

153. 龙 lóng / 4.1

154. 路 lù / 8.1

155. 旅行 lǚxíng / 7.1

156. 妈妈 māma / 3.1

157. 马路 mǎlù / 8.1

158. 吗 ma / 1.1

159. 买 mǎi / 5.1

160. 卖 mài / 5.1

161. 忙 máng / 6.2

162. 没关系 méi guānxi / 6.2

163. 没有 méiyǒu / 3.2

164. 每 měi / 7.2

165. 门口 ménkǒu / 8.2

166. 们 men / 1.1

167. 米饭 mǐfàn / 5.2

168. 名字 míngzi / 1.1

169. 明天 míngtiān / 6.1

170. 哪 nǎ / 1.1

171. 哪儿（哪里）nǎr (nǎlǐ) /
   2.2

172. 哪国人 nǎ guó rén / 1.1

173. 那 nà / 2.2

174. 那 nà / 5.1

175. 那儿（那里）nàr (nàlǐ) /
   3.2

176. 男 nán / 2.2

177. 男孩儿 nánháir / 3.1

178. 呢 ne / 1.1

179. 能 néng / 4.2

180. 你 nǐ / 1.1

181. 您 nín / 1.2

182. 您贵姓 nín guìxìng / 1.2

183. 牛 niú / 5.2

184. 牛肉 niúròu / 5.2

185. 牛仔裤 niúzǎikù / 7.2

186. 女 nǚ / 2.2

187. 女孩儿 nǚháir / 3.1

188. 哦 ò / 7.2

189. 旁边 pángbiān / 8.1

190. 朋友 péngyou / 2.2

191. 皮肤 pífū / 7.2

192. 漂亮 piàoliang / 2.2

193. 七 qī / 0

194. 骑 qí / 8.2

195. 汽车 qìchē / 8.2

196. 千 qiān / 3.2

197. 前面（前边）qiánmiàn
   (qiánbian) / 8.1

198. 钱 qián / 5.1

199. 请 qǐng / 2.2
200. 请问 qǐngwèn / 4.2
201. 球 qiú / 6.1
202. 去 qù / 3.2
203. 然后 ránhòu / 8.2
204. 让 ràng / 3.2
205. 人 rén / 1.1
206. 认识 rènshi / 2.1
207. 肉 ròu / 5.2
208. 三 sān / 0
209. 山 shān / 4.1
210. 商店 shāngdiàn / 5.1
211. 上车 shàng chē / 8.2
212. 上课 shàngkè / 4.2
213. 上面（上边）shàngmiàn
     (shàngbian) / 8.1
214. 上午 shàngwǔ / 6.1
215. 上旬 shàngxún / 7.1
216. 烧 shāo / 5.2
217. 少 shǎo / 3.2
218. 十 shí / 0
219. 什么 shénme / 1.1
220. 什么时候 shénme shíhou /
     6.2
221. 时候 shíhou / 6.2
222. 市 shì / 8.2
223. 市中心 shì zhōngxīn / 8.2
224. 事儿 shìr / 6.2
225. 试 shì / 5.1
226. 是 shì / 1.1
227. 是的 shì de / 2.1
228. 瘦 shòu / 7.2
229. 书 shū / 4.2
230. 蔬菜 shūcài / 5.2
231. 谁 shéi/shuí / 4.2
232. 水饺（饺子）shuǐjiǎo
     (jiǎozi) / 5.2

233. 说 shuō / 1.2
234. 四 sì / 0
235. 酸 suān / 5.2
236. 酸辣汤 suānlàtāng / 5.2
237. 岁 suì / 3.1
238. 他 tā / 1.1
239. 太 tài / 5.1
240. 太……了！ tài…le / 5.1
241. 太太 tàitai / 3.1
242. 汤 tāng / 5.2
243. 糖 táng / 5.2
244. 糖醋鱼 tángcùyú / 5.2
245. 条 tiáo / 5.1
246. 同学 tóngxué / 1.2
247. 头发 tóufa / 7.2
248. 外面（外边）wàimiàn
     (wàibian) / 8.1
249. 玩儿 wánr / 4.1
250. 晚上 wǎnshang / 6.1
251. 万 wàn / 3.2
252. 往 wǎng / 8.1
253. 为 wèi / 3.2
254. 为什么 wèi shénme / 3.2
255. 位 wèi / 6.2
256. 问 wèn / 4.2
257. 我 wǒ / 1.1
258. 五 wǔ / 0
259. 喜欢 xǐhuan / 2.2
260. 系 xì / 2.2
261. 下车 xià chē / 8.2
262. 下面（下边）xiàmiàn
     (xiàbian) / 8.1
263. 下午 xiàwǔ / 6.1
264. 下旬 xiàxún / 7.1
265. 先 xiān / 8.2
266. 先生 xiānsheng / 3.1
267. 现在 xiànzài / 6.2

268. 想 xiǎng / 3.2
269. 小 xiǎo / 2.2
270. 谢谢 xièxie / 2.1
271. 星期 xīngqī / 6.1
272. 星期六 xīngqīliù / 6.1
273. 行 xíng / 4.1
274. 行人 xíngrén / 8.1
275. 姓 xìng / 1.2
276. 休息 xiūxi / 6.1
277. 学生 xuésheng / 3.2
278. 学习 xuéxí / 2.2
279. 学校 xuéxiào / 3.2
280. 学院 xuéyuàn / 2.2
281. 眼镜 yǎnjìng / 7.2
282. 要 yào / 4.1
283. 也 yě / 1.1
284. 一 yī / 0
285. 一点儿 yìdiǎnr / 5.1
286. 一会儿 yíhuìr / 7.2
287. 一起 yìqǐ / 6.1
288. 一下 yíxià / 4.1
289. 衣服 yīfu / 5.1
290. 以后 yǐhòu / 7.1
291. 以前 yǐqián / 7.1
292. 意思 yìsi / 4.1
293. 因为 yīnwèi / 3.2
294. 银行 yínháng / 8.1
295. 英汉词典 Yīng-Hàn cídiǎn /
     4.2
296. 英文 Yīngwén / 4.1
297. 英语 Yīngyǔ / 1.2
298. 营业 yíngyè / 5.1
299. 营业员 yíngyèyuán / 5.1
300. 用 yòng / 4.2
301. 邮件 yóujiàn / 2.1
302. 邮局 yóujú / 8.1
303. 有 yǒu / 3.1

语法项目索引 Index of Grammatical Items

功能项目索引 Index of Functional Items

责任编辑：韩 颖 付 眉
英文编辑：韩芙芸
封面设计：Daniel Gutierrez
插　图：笑 龙

图书在版编目（CIP）数据

当代中文.课本.1：汉英对照/吴中伟主编.—修订版.—北京：华语教学出版社，2014

ISBN 978-7-5138-0617-6

I.①当… II.①吴… III.①汉语－对外汉语教学－教材 IV.① H195.4

中国版本图书馆 CIP 数据核字 (2013) 第 292939 号

当代中文

课本

1

主编　吴中伟

*

© 华语教学出版社有限责任公司

华语教学出版社有限责任公司出版

（中国北京百万庄大街 24 号 邮政编码 100037）

电话：(86)10-68320585, 68997826

传真：(86)10-68997826, 68326333

网址：www.sinolingua.com.cn

电子信箱：hyjx@sinolingua.com.cn

新浪微博地址：http://weibo.com/sinolinguavip

北京密兴印刷有限公司印刷

2003 年（16 开）第 1 版

2014 年（16 开）修订版

2019 年修订版第 7 次印刷

（汉英）

ISBN 978-7-5138-0617-6

定价：69.00 元